Football Book

Football Strategies: Understand How To Watch The Game And Learn Tactics And Rules Of How They Play Football To Win

CONTENTS

Preamble

"Ronny Run," Irving the Coach of a small town American Football team making first appearance of the season cried out his voice reverberating in the stadium breaking the silence which span the well attended match as rain peppered the roof and seconds ticked away in the game. A spectator in the crowd picked up and echoed Irving's sentiments. The sold out stadium crowd joined in the foray of the unmistakable sound of chant encouraging "Ronny Run," with renewed enthusiasm.

Ronny cupped the ball in his left hand, his right hand fended opponents with ferocity as the legs pounded the ground in a hundred meter sprint heading towards end zone. You could see pebbles of sweat on close up shot of his face on the giant screens mounted in four strategic corners in the stadium.

You couldn't tell who the opponents were from shouts in the crowd urging Ronny to run and reach the end zone before time lapse in the final quarter of the game.

The two teams were running neck to neck on scores as the neon stop clock mounted high on the wall of the stadium began the last minute countdown 60, 59, 58, 57…. Anything could go wrong at this crucial point of time in the game. If there is such a thing as superstition, this is not the time and place for it. Will Ronny live up to the crowd's expectation? The outcome of this game hinged on the balance of ten factors outlined in this book. This book brings you up to date on

- How Football Field is Set Up
- How Rules and Regulations Govern American Football
- How Equipment Used in the Game Protects Players

- How Strategy Works for Win
- How Tricks & Techniques Change the Course of Direction in the Match
- How Players Attitude Influence Outcome of the Game
- How Different Super Bowl Champions were Played and Won in the Pas
- How Other Individuals Contribute to the Success of the Game

INTRODUCTION

I want to thank you and congratulate you for downloading the book, "Football Book: Football Strategies: Understand How To Watch The Game And Learn Tactics And Rules Of How They Play Football To Win".

This book has comprehensive information about football.

Super Bowl tournament in New York might be as far removed from European football cup finals in Wimbledon as Las Vegas is from Lagos, but the game generates excitement, elation and chronic disappointment in equal measure no matter where you're and at what level it is played. That initial magnetic attraction remains undiminished in high school, college and super bowl tournaments.

What is the difference between high school, college and NLF Super bowl? Which of these three levels of the game present more appeal? Does this game remind you of unfulfilled promise of failing to make the team selection to advance playing in the season? How well do you understand the challenges players of this game go through in the field? These are legitimate significant questions anyone keen on following football as a sport or are passionate about career in this game need to ask in order to get more acquainted with the game.

You probably don't understand why men in helmets are running each other down scrambling to get a hold of the ball in play. Why do they attack each other violently? Well, do not let painful memories of the last high school, college football or Super Bowl rob you of the joy of enjoying many more football games yet to be played in the history of this game. Whether you're a spectator, coach, official of the game, amateur or professional player of football game; this books shows you all you need to know to enjoy the game.

Today American football is one of top ten sports played around the world and its gaining popularity with the advent of advance technology as a trendy game. Muscles twitch, sweat flows as men compete to gain control of the ball in this game.

Whenever two teams make their way onto a football field, you can expect fireworks. No team advance in the game without claiming every single inch in the field if against the other team if possible. The offense is rearing to break defense guarded goal line and the defense is all eyes leaving nothing to chance to prevent the offense from infiltration during the game.

The ultimate aim is to gain sufficient ground to land a field goal or touchdown. This book teaches you how points are scored, the field, and various positions. In addition you learn professional football rules. But that is not all. This book also covers basic defense and offense strategies in chapter four. .

Thanks again for downloading this book, I hope you enjoy it!

Today American football is one of top ten sports played around the world and its gaining popularity with the advent of advance technology as a trendy game. Muscles twitch, sweat flows as men compete to gain control of the ball in this game.

Whenever two teams make their way onto a football field, you can expect fireworks. No team advance in the game without claiming every single inch in the field if against the other team if possible. The offense is rearing to break defense guarded goal line and the defense is all eyes leaving nothing to chance to prevent the offense from infiltration during the game.

The ultimate aim is to gain sufficient ground to land a field goal or touchdown. This book teaches you how points are scored, the field, and various positions. In addition you learn professional football rules. But that is not all. This book also covers basic defense and offense strategies in chapter four. .

Thanks again for downloading this book, I hope you enjoy it!

Chapter One

THE FOOTBALL FIELD

An average field is approximately one hundred yards in length and one hundred and sixty yards in width. There are lines at every ten yards to signal how far either team needs to go before they reach the end zones. These lines are included at both ends of the field and have an approximate length of twenty yards.

Twenty two players occupy the field during the game. The twenty two consist of 11 players from each team. The referee is in the game in his capacity as the official and does not take part in the game in any other way.

A typical American football team is made up of forty five players, categorized into 3 attacking groups (faster, smaller, stronger kind of players, comprising a quarterback, whose responsibility includes throwing the ball to his teammates and running the attacking plays), defense (more powerful and larger players meant to prevent players from running), as well as special team players (who kick and punt the side of the game, and comprise faster and larger players). A professional football field is characterized by seven prominent features.

However, action in the game focuses on the individual and the ball. That is reason for the emphasis of individual player's participation in chapter six. However, individual player is not the only one involved in the game. Football would be incomplete without the coach, team doctor, ball boys, sports writer and spectators. Chapter 8 gives prominence to the individuals working behind the scene to make this game a success.

Seven Prominent Features on Football Field

1. Goal Posts – Goal posts are made of 10 feet long steel planted at the back of the end zone on the ground and secured by concrete, in the middle to support two towering vertical extensions that rise to a height of thirty feet above the ground. Goal post extensions go up eighteen-feet and have six inch cross bar at the base of the posts. The two upright extensions feature a red ribbon tied at the top, ideally 10cm by 107cm.

2. Hash marks and Yard Lines – Hash marks are located within the one hundred yards between goal lines on both sides of the field to mark every yard. There is a solid white line running from sideline to sideline at every 5th yards, which are numbered after every ten yards. The gridiron nickname derives its meaning from this pattern of lines.

3. Goal Line – This eight inch wide line running across the anterior of the end zone is the last point of the goal line. It is flanked by two pylons.

4. End Zone – Two ten yard wide regions at every end of the field within the end line are set aside as end zone. A team's end zone is the end zone behind it.

5. End Line – this is a six foot wide line that marks the boundary between 2 parallel sidelines. The field's rectangular shape is composed of the sideline and the end line. The last point of the end line is flanked by two pylons.

6. Sideline – this is the six-foot wide line stretch which marks the boundary between the lengths of the football field.

7. The ball is the most significant part of a football game

American Footballs comes in different shapes and sizes providing variety in high school, college and professional football game. Over the years different materials have been tested and tried in making the ball. These materials range from bladders, hides, rubber, paint leather and string among others. Football has maintained its original oblong shape with slight variations from the first ball thrown in 1860.

Official NFL ball weighs 12.5 to 13.5 lbs inclusive of material weight of 14-15 oz before the ball is inflated. This is the standard weight and air pressure required for the ball across the board.

Next take along hard look at the field and notice that it is marked starting from one end to the next and on both sides. The bold marks are not for decorations. But you don't need to memorize what each line is called so what if one is called yard line and the other scrimmage line and another end zone.

The reason you go to watch football match is to see individual players brilliant run to score a whooping six points on touchdown. That is what gets the crowd up on their feet to cheer wildly not the lines and not the positions or kick offs but scores.

Football

The material for making football consists of four measured and weighed leather panels inspected before being sewn for blemishes. The two top panels are put together with white leather laces. Inserted inside the leather panels is a 3 ply VPU rubber bladder for holding air when the ball is inflated.

Home clubs supply 36 balls for the big NFL games during outdoor contests and 24 for indoor games respectively. In addition to the number of indoor or outdoor games 12 balls are marked letter "K," are used specifically for kick offs. The referee ensures the balls are the right sizes, weight and have the required air pressure pumped inside them.

Football was made of pig skin in the early days of the game. Rubber came along as a new development to replace the pig skin. However, with time and search for official standard, the ball is now made from genuine water resistant leather for use in diverse cold weather conditions.

Wilson Sporting Goods Co. provides handmade official NFL footballs, which are oblong spheres that are between 11 and 11.5 inches long. They have lengthwise circumferences of approximately 72.4 cm or 28.5 inches and widthwise circumferences of approximately 54.6cm or 21.5 inches at the center of the football. It has a weight of 14 to 15 ounces, and is made up of a polyurethane bladder, which is inflated and protected by cowhide covering.

Gridcord material is used to lace the ball, which is basically cotton thread coated with vinyl. The inside of the leather covering is sewn using a 3ply, synthetic lining to provide additional protection to the bladder and helps maintain the distinct and elongated shape of the football. A valve is also linked to the bladder, protruding through the leather to facilitate pumping of air into the ball.

Now you're up to date with basic understanding of the football field. The next important step is to be aware of the rules and regulations of the game. Let's get down to rules and regulations that govern this game.

Summary

Football field has specific measurement, one hundred yards in length and one hundred and sixty yards in width. In addition to the measurement of the field in this chapter are the seven prominent features on the pitch namely, goal posts, harsh marks, goal line, end zone, end line, side line, and the ball.

Chapter 2

AMERICAN FOOTBALL RULES & REGULATIONS

Ronny sensed the pressure and squeeze on time. He lifted his eyes to the score board wall clock holding the back pass ball. You couldn't tell if he was calculating the remaining seconds to make a run with it to the end zone or give it a good kick half way down the pitch aiming at opponent's goal posts.

Even if Ronny runs to touch down (which was highly unlikely in less than 60 seconds), will he hand victory to his team in the dying minutes of the game?

All competitive games have rules and regulations governing the match and safeguarding players in the game. You don't need to know all the rules to play or watch the game. But you do need basic understanding to follow and enjoy the game. How would you know if the nose tackle is savage or safe on the offense?

Albert Einstein said, "Information is important than fact." Football boasts of more rules than any other game in comparison. These rules are in five set categories feature shared, structure, scoring, starting and on stage rules in the game during play time. Let's take a look at each of the fourteen single rules in the five sets categories and the officials of the game charged with responsibility to ensure that these rules and regulations are kept to the letter.

General Rules of the Game

1. A typical football game consists of 4 fifteen minute quarters. In addition, there is a two-minute break after the first and third quarters, as well as a fifteen-minute rest period between the second and third quarters.

2. The two competing teams are given four downs or chances to gain ten or more yards, in the field. This the team can achieve by either running or throwing the ball. Both the yardage and the downs are reset when a team achieves the necessary yards. On the other hand, if after the four downs the team fails to achieve the yardage, the game results in a turnover.

3. Players can use any of the different numerous plays to run on any chance (down). The teams make up the plays, which involves the players running around in the field after the ball. The quarter back or the head coach is responsible for calling the on field plays.

4. A coin is tossed before any game begins to determine the team that will start attacking, as well as the side of the field they choose at the beginning of the game.

5. A kick off signals the start of the game, where one team strikes the ball down field and the other runs back as far as possible with the ball.

6. There are two possibilities for the offence when they reach 4th down: they can either kick the ball or try to compensate for the yards they need. I the team choose the former alternative; the team either attempts a field goal or decides to punt. The position on the field will often determine the play. The team attempts to score a field goal if they are within forty or so yards of the other side's goal posts. However, if they are further back, they are better off taking the punt alternative.

Starting Game Rules

The second set of football rules focus on starting the game. Two rules observed in this category are the coin toss and kick off.

Rule 1: Coin Flip – Coin flip determines kick off at the start of the game. Each session in the game starts with the winning team taking the kick off. In addition to the 3 minute break in case of tie at the end of normal playtime. There are two minute interval breaks for each team to score in the absence of touchdown in the extra time in the game.

Rule2: Kick Off – On kick off, the ball floats on air from offense to defense side. The defense is on hand to catch the ball and make a run with it towards the kicking team's goals. The kicking team pursuing scores want to advance position of the ball in play. The two teams will battle for the oval shaped ball made out of skin for durability and well maintained for play. Members of the two teams are on the lookout for loop holes in the other team's field position to break through.

The defense kicks the ball to offense during kick to start the game, second half and when points are scored in the game.

Game Structure Rules

Third set of three rules govern structure of the game

Rule 3: Circumference

Football game is played in a designated area on the field. Chapter one highlights the demarcation of the field and how each section functions in the game.

Rule 4: Contenders

Two teams take part in the game with equal number of 11 players each team. This is a non negotiable rule.

Rule 5: Coverage of the game

The full time in the game is set for sixty minutes of fifteen minute segments known as quarters. This time line varies due to time outs, kick-offs, penalty shootouts and other activities that make football game.

Scoring Points Rules

Fourth set of rules regulate scoring points in the game

Rule 6: Touchdown is the maximum score of six rule awarded when the ball is thrown moved by offense and placed down on the opponents' end zone.

Rule 7: Extra Points Awarded for Touchdown

This rule benefits the team that scores six points on touchdown. The team is given the opportunity to score additional one point through a kick calculated to pass between the goal posts, a thro or when the ball is literally carried by the team to opponents' end zone.

Rule 8: Field Goal —

The attacking players can score a field goal from any point on the field and at any time, with a successful kick. This type of kick is earns the team 3 points. The point where an attacking player is tackled successfully by the defensive team in their own end zone is known as a safety, which is worth two points.

Rule 9: Safety Rule

In the event the offense player with the ball stuck in his end zone is tackled by defense player, the defense gets awarded two points. This is one unusual football rule, yet it scores points for the defense.

Game Play Rules

Fifth set of football rules preside over the game. There four rules in this category revolve around ball handing, downs, barring, out of bounds, five yard intervals all in happening during ball movement.

Rule 10: Ball Possession –

The team with the ball at any point in the game has possession.

Failure by offense to move the ball forward gives the defense chance of ball possession in the game.

Rule 11:

Offense fails to move the ball after four required ten yard downs turn the ball to defense. The offense becomes the defense.

Rule 12:

Fourth down awarded offense to kick the ball to the opponent who failed to advance the ball in the game.

Rule 13: 10 second run off rule

In the absence of these commons dozen rules in the game, offensive team without time out remaining in the game could deliberately commit an offense to derail and buy time to stay in the lead to the end of the end. The team could spike or throw the ball from the field of play to stop the clock. In return the team is punished with loss of yards. This tactic allows teams to stop the clock in the dying minutes of the game without using time out to run one last play calculated to seal their lead in the match.

Rule 14: Out of Bounds Rule

American Football is arguably one of the most significant sports in North America. While the game is now played worldwide, the North American professional leagues like the NFL attract the most efficient players in the world. This makes it the most competitive game in the United States of America and neighboring Canada.

The highpoint of the game is the Super Bowl, which is played out to millions of people across the globe every year live via simultaneous broadcast telecast on electronic media – television and radio.

Game Officials

NFL games are supervised by 3-7 member crew officials. These officials include:-

1. Referee – In charge of the game.
2. Umpire responsible for handling spotting the ball.
3. Head Linesmen who see to the placement of down box
4. Line Judge
5. Back Judge
6. Side Judge.

These officials are vetted and selected by the competing teams. NFL is in the process of implementing a policy system that will include the 7 officials as permanent employees.

This action would take the shape of major leagues as Basketball, NBA and NHL leagues.

American Football game officials get rely on administrative help from:-

- Clock Operator
- Chair Crew – Taking measurement to settle replay disputes in the game.
- Ball Boys – Run the length and width of field to fetch an get

the ball back to player. Some of the boys are on hand to supply extra ball on time for the game to continue without unnecessary delays.

Summary

The five sets of football rules and regulations outlined in this chapter feature general, starting, game structure and scoring rules. Anyone keen on this game can comfortably get along with the 14 most common sing rules and regulations in the five sets discussed in this chapter.

In addition, the chapter highlights the role of game officials.

Chapter Three

HOW EQUIPMENT USED IN THE GAME PROTECTS PLAYERS

Television and radio maintenance technicians have plastic foam tape item in the tool box to seal off holes in the circuit during repair. Plastic sealing tape consists of polyether foam plastic laminated to a high strength rope paper backing which incorporates a firm bond high tack adhesive.

This adhesive is protected by an easy to remove paper inter-liner and the tape is fixed on position by stripping back the inter-liner and applying firm finger pressure to the plastic foam. Not only does this adhesive provide a first class seal, it has ideal vibration and shock resistance characteristics. It can also be used as a gasket around television component parts where protection against vibration and dust is vital.

The nature of American Football requires that players wear protective gear to minimize the rate of injury to the body. This chapter lists and explains how football equipment is used and the important role the gear plays to protect the player. Here is the top ten list of recommended protective equipment necessary in American Football game.

Top Ten List of Recommended Protective Gear

1. **Helmet** – Protects the head on hard knock and head butting which could cause concussions and damage the brain.

Head injuries on collision courses during the game could result in irreparable brain damage. Thanks to the head gear and shoulders. While scrambling for the ball, opponents' savage attack could impair the other permanently without the gears worn during the game.

Human brain is sensitive and central to the working system of the body, it needs all the protection. Helmet shell is made to match body contact and ensure the player of full protection of vulnerable parts of the head. It is made with pads to protect the jaw and, face mask and chin strap among its functional parts.

Helmet is the No. 1 gear required in football game and worn all the time during play for protection. It has metal bars and chin strap to secure it to the head. The rest of the parts are additional protective pieces. Your teeth could rattle, jaws locked through hard know in the game without this head protection. Helmets are made to match different player head sizes by measuring the head of each player with clippers. The helmet is padded with foam, rubber and inflatable air pads. Although the helmet is made of metal, all necessary precautions are taken to ensure it light enough and easy on the head for action.

When a player ears are all covered up in the helmet, the only way to make contact and communication is through radio dummies fitted to the helmet. Small speakers are fitted on each side of the ears on the helmet to aid hearing.

Quarter back, Coach, Offense coordinators communicate with players through radio signals during the game. Quality of sound is good during reception in isolation but not so good in crowded places but that is a small price to pay for small inconvenience in reception.

The crowd noise could muffle sound quality making it difficult but not impossible to accomplish the task 100%. But then again without the crowd noise, the game of football would be dull and boring. Visor is the latest addition to the helmet for eye protection.

2. **Shoulder Pads** – Players rub shoulders with one another all the time the game. It not surprising the applied force could be put your shoulder out of joint, reason you need it wrapped with pads to cushion the hard tackles and falls during the game.

Shoulder pads are made of hard plastic shell with shock absorbers from padding underlay. Shoulder pads cover the shoulder, ch est and rib in addition to areas of the body prone to injury during contact on attacks by opponents in the game. Players' look a little off shape with wide broad unnatural shoulders wearing shoulder pads but two benefits of wearing these pads stand out.

- Shoulder pads absorb hard tackle shocks to the body which defines the game of football.
- Spread out the shock so the impact is not concentrated in an area, enough to cause great damage to the body part in contact.

3. **Gloves** – Hands are vulnerable to injury. Hands grab the ball, body parts and maintain balance during running in the game. In case of a fall your hand gets to the ground first.

If the hand lands on a sharp object without gloves, the hand could get a serious cut on contact with the object or bruised from a fall on hard ground. Gloves with sticky rubber are used by players to protect the hands and assist in trapping sliding balls. However, gels are disallowed to use.

4. **Footwear** – Non slip material for soles of boots and shoes with outer layer containing steel fibers dispersed in rubber were developed and have been used for many years.

A player needs a good pair of shoes to protect the feet, apply the brakes and quicken his span to put distance between him and ensuing opponent in the battle over the ball. Football footwear has soles with spikes tailor made for guys' games on grass. Special footwear has removable screw on/off cleats used in case the sole is damaged but the shoe body is still intact.

5. Thigh and Knee Pads

American Football is a rough game for rough men. The knee is the most widely used part of the body in the game as it also comes in contact with other players body parts.

Normal knee is aligned so that a straight line drawn from the centre of the hip joint toward the center of the ankle joint that passes directly through the center of the knee join.

When your knee joints are in this proper alignment, the force generated across will be distributed equally to support the body with the help of meniscus over a wider surface area in each compartment.

If you've 150 pounds body weight, you generate 450 pounds of force, merely by walking! That weight is supported by the knee. Knowing this could stimulate your need to protect the knee during football game.

The knee joint is not a simple ball-and-socket affair like the hip joint, which is probably why it takes long to heal in case of injury during the game.

6. Hip Pads

Dislocation of hip shoulders, are common among football players. You have to be fit as a fiddle to accommodate the full force exerted by opponents determined to stop you dead on your tracks and prevent you from getting anywhere near the end zone using every nook and crook of tricks in the bags.

7. Tailbone Pads

8. Rib Pads

Players are better place for safety wearing all this gear in the game. That is a lot of weight to haul around and run along with strapped to your body. While every last one of football equipment is necessary, players have a choice to pick on the best and most essential pieces mandatory for the game. Football regimen equipment is not complete without Jockstrap, Jerseys and Pants.

9. Jockstrap –

Male organ is the most sensitive and vulnerable part of the body. Imagine an opponent treading on your peaches. You would hear ear piercing cry not know among men in the field. That would be pain per excellence. Thanks to forward lovers of football game. Jockstrap was introduced to football to protect and contain the genitals in a pouch padded with impact resistant material to minimize injury to male organs.

10. Jersey and Pants

Sportswear form part of the fashion industry in that field. Players patch sportswear material made of nylon to the body with 2 sided carpet tape to keep it down on the body. Players can change Jerseys at half time if it rains during game time. Insignia such as the

American flag, team logo, information in support of the team, manufacturing company of the sportswear, airlines, all scramble for the piece of pie in advertising are common features on players Jerseys.

Pants are made of nylon to match the jerseys with an additional spandex to cling to the body in favorite team colors. Pants have pockets to hold knee cap pads. You don't want pads flying or getting lost in the maze.

Celebrity Sports clothes are collectibles antiques that could be auctioned for cash to raise additional funds for the player even long after leaving the field.

Other Protective Gear

Players value protection of all body parts during the game use additional equipment. Mouth protective gear prevents your teeth from falling off in case you use dentures. You also don't want to walk around with swollen lips after the game from a hard tackle that damage the lips.

Players who put premium on safety also have access to nose guard. You don't have to fear that someone will put your nose out of joint in the game. In addition to the ten mentioned above, protective equipment is mandatory in American Football. You don't have to use all of them but you do need to use basic gear during the game. This equipment has to be well managed and maintained by a manage who takes care of the gear to make sure

- Each player has an array of assortment of necessary equipment.
- Keep tab on easy access and supply of the equipment before during and after the game.

Summary

If you think thirteen is unlucky number, you would shy away from using all the necessary equipment in American Football game discussed in this chapter. Although the ten gears are prominently used and are mandatory, the three optional gears making the number thirteen are just as important for protection in the game.

Chapter Four

HOW STRATEGY WORKS FOR WIN IN FOOTBALL

You don't associate playing football with math, but mathematics forms an integral part of playing football in determining position in the game. You realize the need for team training and capacity building outside the field of play using square numbers, presentation materials, video clips, photos, graphs, charts and other visuals the team can draw tips and techniques from.

Outside the field training aims at prompting players to understand the place of strategy in the game. If you can manage to juggle the square numbers in the box, you're able to use similar strategy in Super Bowl game. This chapter emphasizes the importance of strategy and shows you how it works in winning football game. Specific to the discussion in this section of the book are five Super Bowl strategies that generate winning in the game. The five strategies are: Practice Makes Perfect, Participation and Performance of Individual Player, Priority Amidst Pressure, Prior Planning, Playtime Reflects Preparation in the Game.

The Offense Side Line Up

Football team is essentially made up of three groups: the special, the defense, and the offense teams, each of these groups are assigned positions and have particular set of skills to carry out the task in the designated area of the field.

The work of the offense is to take the ball down the pitch towards the end zone of their opponents. The team can do this by holding the ball and running forward or by passing the ball from player to player. Here is the usual offensive position line up.

- Running Backs – are responsible for receiving the ball from the quarterback, and then run up the pitch with it in the direction of choice. A running back can also be referred to as a fullback (FB), halfback (HB), or tailback (TB), depending on the arrangement or formation of the offensive players.
- Receivers – The receivers are known for running down the pitch and catching the balls passed by the quarterback. Depending on their position on the field, they can be either tight ends (RTE/LTE) or wide receivers (WR).
- Offensive linemen – these are the players responsible for blocking both the running backs and the quarterback. Their individual positions include tackles (RT/LT), guards (RG/LG), and center. The Center is positioned at the center of the line and is responsible for hiking the ball towards the quarterback by bringing it between his legs. The Center is flanked by the Guards and Tackles located on the outside of every guard. There are usually two tackles and two guards in every team.
- Quarterback (QB) –Quarterback is referred to as the field general, since he is the leader of the team on the field. This player hands the ball to running backs or throws it off to the receivers.

Movement of the Ball During Play

The main objective of this game is to end up with the highest point in the allotted time over the opponents. This can be achieved by moving the ball in phases of play down the pitch, before ultimately reaching the end zone to score a touchdown. Players do this by either running with the football or throwing it to a teammate.

The two teams are given four chances to move the football ten yards forward. Once a team passes the ten yards, their chances or downs are reset, which means they can restart for ten more yards. In case they fail to make it across the required ten yards, the ball is handed over to the defensive side. The offense uses five significant strategies to advance the ball with this line in the team.

Five Significant Super Bowl Strategies

Teams use computer where numbers are picked, rows and columns are assigned randomly in the 0-9 digit range of numbers. The main point in this exercise is to figure out up to 60 different configurations available for selection in the game square numbers.

In playing around with these numbers, you lean strategy which is critical in winning American football game. Although in the final analysis, strategy doesn't guarantee expected outcome, it gives probabilities which influence the outcome in the real game.

You can draw a number of parallels between square game numbers and Super Bowl tournament. Here are five Super Bowl strategies that generate winning in the game.

1. **"Practice makes Perfect,"** isn't just an old tired overused cliché in the English language. These three words hold the key to winning or losing in football game. No one knows the profound meaning behind these words better than Coach Vince Lombardi.

"Practice doesn't make perfect. Perfect makes practice." A play on this phrase no doubt but with deeper meaning and insight. Individual Super Bowl players are created perfect in physical, psychological and spiritual ways in every sense of this phrase.

If you attribute meaning of words from scripture – the Bible, Vince Lombardi's proposition come as no surprise. Taking the cue from the Bible reference on the story of Gideon discussed in the next point, it goes without say that a perfect player should practice, practice and practice more to perfect his perfection. Practice is the outward demonstration of the inner ability to excel in sporting events. The potential is inherent within the individual. Practice assists to unleash that potential in the field of football.

The process and procedure of becoming a champion could take a little time. Just as building a lifetime career does. But the outcome is guaranteed if individual team members practice enough with the coach's guidance and share a common purpose to win the game. Together, repeatedly, individual players practice drills over long periods of time to synchronize collective participation in the game. .

2. **Participation and Performance of Individual Player in the Game**

The story of Gideon recorded in the Bible, book of Judges, shows exemplary leadership quality by Gideon to create a winning team for the chosen nation of God the Israelites. The presence of Divine guidance and intervention is evidence in choosing men to go to war against the heathen nations.

However, Gideon's human leadership ability plays a big role in the success of the outcome of these assaults. He took charge of the army, initiated cooperation of ten men to lead the delegations to war.

You've read and heard of practical experiences in history of men and women with rare leadership abilities that spearheaded and led great exploits for victories in different fields. These individuals did not have to literally fight, but became change agents in fostering unity and influencing the outcome of events in the war. Here is an example from the Battle of Alamo.

- **Battle of Alamo**

In December 1835, mutinous Texans took control of the city of Antonio de Béxar. Mexican General Santa Anna in charge of defense cordoned the fortified Alamo and led the attack.

The Texans weren't supposed to be there
Tension was high as some officers considered surrender. Many supported the attack, while the rest were undecided. Ben Milan called the indecision to order. He had good reason having fought for Mexico against Spain.

On March 6, the Battle of Alamo reached its peak. Texan rifles blazed, cannons exploded as Mexican headed towards fortified Alamo. In the end, Alamo fell within 90 minutes of attack.

This Battle of Alamo has gone down in history with names of men who took centre stage as Crockett, Bowie, Travis and Bonham curving a niche in the history books. A number of movies have been made on the battle and the historical books written on the events testify to the Texans resilience under enormous pressure and minority in numbers to rise to the occasion during this war. Football is a grueling task similar in nature to war fought by individuals in the army. The outcome of the war depends on individual as well collective participation of the army much the same as in football.

- **Individual and Collective Members Participation in the Game**

Individual player's brilliant performance in the game does not guarantee the team wins. Quarter back, the main man of the moment in the match depends on the support of 5 Offense Linesmen, 2 Side Receivers, I Running Back, 1 Full Back and 1 Tight End. Together this crew in the eleven players' football squad works to advance the ball towards the opponents' end zone.

The Quarter back can't single handedly run the ball and score without the help of team mates. True, there have been cases in extreme situations where individual players in the game such as Ronny saved the team from a humiliating defeat with a dare devil run to score six points on touchdown putting the team on the lead in the dying minutes of the game. While such cases happen, they're the exceptions rather than the norms. In a normal situation, team work carries the day to ease off pressure on individual players.

3. Priority Amidst Pressure in Participation

How does a team leading in scores maintain the lead in the game? A number of issues come into sharp focus in this consideration. Time management is on top of the priority list of issues each team deals with in the game. Time is essential during play time. Time management takes different forms depending on the position of the team in the game during playtime.

Another area of priority amidst pressure is on related activities to the game which nibble on game time allocated. Practice time is precious and so is play and performance. Practice goes beyond drill to visualization of the outcome of the game. Visualizing the outcome is individual and collective team's choice.

Timeout, one of the avenues for reconstruction of play pattern is an opportunity that cannot miss mentioning in considering priority amidst pressure in the game. All these activities pile up pressure on individual, team, and the Coach to prioritize.

The aim is to cease opportunity of taking and maintaining the lead to the end of the game by one team. It is race against time and every individual player's input and participation counts in the final analysis.

That is also the reason teams keen to win enlist assistance of motivational speakers to assist with psychological aspect of individual team member's attitude in the game. Physical apart from psychological is not enough. Players need their success steam cranked up as top priority for peak performance.

4. Prior Planning Precedes Perfect Performances

You don't wake up one day and decide to take part in Super Bowl competition. In your dreams that could happen. In real life, it take careful planning involving five member crew officials to pull off the game between two opposing teams of 11 players, coaches and subordinate staff of the teams.

No team will allow you anywhere near the game. The Coach won't hear a word of it no matter how convincing you're. The team plans the game in advance with players in attendance. If you're absent from planning sessions, you're not part of the playing squad in the team during the tournament.

Teams set aside time for practice, review videos clips on the game, study different situations and activities of the game, kick offs, penalties, passes and all else that goes into making the game a success. In the process, the coach points out pitfalls on passes, runs, kick offs that could cost the team much needed touch down six points to stay in the lead or even out scores in the game.

Planning takes into account study of the pattern of play winning teams' use. If the team can't match set standards, the alternative is to model the style of play and the team is on its way to winning the much talked about Super Bowl championship tournament of the season.

5. Playtime Mirrors Individual and Collective Players Preparation

The Coach does his best to provide players with tips and techniques in the game through charts, photos, video clips demonstrating ball placement, kick offs, runs, but the individual player is responsible to carry out and execute the action in the real game.

The Coach works hand in hand with the team prior and during the game remotely. He shouts himself hoarse when players in the team are not coordinating in the game to yield tangible results. There is nothing more the coach can do except watch and wait for the final outcome of the game in that case.

"You can take the cow to the river but you can't force the cow to drink water," one old African proverb says. The honor is placed on individual as well as the shoulder of the team. How badly does the team want to win depend on the premium the side places on winning the game?

- **Strategy for Scoring is met with Strict Opponent's Resistance.**

Mounting touchdown strategy by one team is met with great resistance by opponents in the game. Defenders are watching the ball with hawk eyes. Offense players are up against head butting, sliding over, pushing and shoving in the scramble for the ball. If none of these works, because the player pulls theatrical run strings to dodge by putting power in the legs to take 3 or more steps at a time, mows opponents standing on the way down to make passage way through, opponents resort to alternative action plan to stop ball movement towards the end zone.

The two teams fight tooth and nail however hard pressed to let the player with the ball pass through with ease. Gaining entrance into opponents' fortified territory with the ball in hand is similar to a doctor performing an operation without ether.

Touchdown provides opportunity for the team to earn extra 1-2 points extra points on trial award, the ball spotted 15 yards for two points and 3 yard line conversion for college and high school football standard. The two point conversion choice has better prospects.

However, the success is less than 40%. But this disadvantage pales in comparison to the advantages this option yields if successful. Here are some of the outstanding benefits from touchdown score.

6. Offense kicks the ball through goal posts in a similar manner to field goal kick. If the kick taken goes through the team gets an extra point awarded in the game.

7. Another alternative benefit from touchdown is that offense runs the ball or advance ball movement through passes from designated places in the same way as in mounting touchdown offensive to score 2 extra points up for grabs during the match.

Win or lose outcome in any competitive game is similar in nature to the two sides of coin. You can't have one without the other. The ultimate outcome is in the mind. Positive mental attitude goes a long way to pave the way for win. Negative mental attitude is the antidote and it plots the loss graph in the play.

Peak performers in all competitive games are passionate about winning. That is what drives and sets them apart from losers. "Quitters never win," you've heard it said. The team motivated by the desire to lift the converted super bowl trophy is determined to exhibit quality performance during the game to win.

In the "The New Dynamics of Winning," Dennis Waitley, emphasis is on mindset of the participants. Chapter six echoes similar sentiments expressed in this book how mental attitude influences the outcome of the game. Be sure to read and reread this chapter for it holds time tested truth on successful football game outcome.

On the ground, strategy doesn't mean much if it is not translated into scoring points. There is also no one fit size for all strategic plans a team can use without making adjustments here and there during the game. But knowing the basics does help to have a head start to upcoming game.

It is one thing to watch and enjoy the game for the excitement it generates. It is another to know the basic rules, strategies in the game. If for nothing else you're keen on gambling on the game which is part and parcel of putting together teams, you need to have adequate information on the game. Gambling on football is fast gaining grounds and those eyeing it from that end would want to know more than the basic to commit money into gambling.

If you have to know all that American football is, the rules, regulations, strategy, and all that goes into play, you could spend a lifetime seeking information and miss out the season's tournament for lack of good grasp on the game.

Don't get bogged down with all the details of football. You know enough already to enjoy the game. The field is no good without players on it. These same players on the street outside the stadium are normal people who also don't know much about your trade and they are not sweating over it. So why should you?

Ball movement shows the offense has upper hand, the reverse indicates the defense have taken over control of the game. It is that simple and straight forward.

Everyone in the stadium have eyes on the player with the ball. That is the offense team. When he is attacked, that the defense in action at the game. It can't be simpler than that. But do not let the simplicity intimidate you to think football is not a rough game for rough men.

The offense is working on more strategies to get past the defense. That does mean the defense is clueless. Not in the very least. The defense could show no signs of strategic plans but don't be fooled into thinking the defense has no strategy to counter the offense onslaught.

Defense and Special Teams

A team is said to be on defense when it does not possess the ball. However, the team uses different strategies to prevent the offense from scoring. The secret is to tackle the player in possession of the ball in order to prevent him gaining grounds in the defense territory. Defense also takes hold of the ball from the advancing players should the offense lose control of it. Defense line up consists of:

- Safeties – Generally, the safeties are positioned deep behind the other defense players in a bid to prevent a run or a long pass. The side of the pitch with more offensive players is accompanied with a strong safety (SS), while the free safety

(FS) occupies a deep and middle position.

- Cornerbacks (CB) – the work of the cornerbacks is to break up the quarterback's passes and prevent them from reaching the receivers.
- Linebackers (LB) – Within 4 linemen are 2 outside linebackers (OLB) and a middle linebacker (MLB). 2 outside linebackers and 2 inside linebackers in this squad provide backup for the linemen, in addition to covering receivers on certain plays and containing runners.
  - Defensive linemen – The work of the linemen is to put pressure on the attacking quarterback and tackle him before he has a chance to release the football. Defense linemen can also try to contain the running backs. Normally, there are 3 or 4 defensive linemen, with individual positions including Tackle (RDT/LDT), Nose tackle (NT), and Ends (LE/RE).

Special Teams

The special teams come into play when the team is given the chance to kick the ball. This unit is made up of the offensive line, the kickers, and players who tackle a returner by running down the pitch on special mission. Think of special teams as task forces called upon to rescue a situation out of control or hand.

- Returner – The returner's work is to try to catch the ball during a punt or kickoff, and then return it as far back as possible. A touchdown can result from a player on a return.
- Punter – the work of the punter is to free kick the ball in case his team fails to move the ball down the pitch.
- Placekicker – This player scores points by kicking the ball through the goalposts.

The main thing is to get the opposition as far away from your half of the field as possible. You can watch and enjoy football with as little knowledge as knowing that the two teams represent the offense and defense in the pitch and when one team is in possession of the ball, the other automatically becomes the defense in the game.

Summary

Individual amateur or professional players' skills improvement draws heavily on different strategies used in football game. This chapter outlines the offense and defense lines up and, highlight Five Significant Super Bowl Strategies and conclude with special mission task forces referred to as special teams in the game.

The five strategies include but not limited to: Practice makes Perfect, Participation and Performance of Individual Player in the Game, Priority Amidst Pressure, Prior Planning Precedes Perfect Performance and Playtime Reflects Preparation

Whether the team is playing high school, college or NFL football the need for strategy in the game cannot be overemphasized.

Chapter Five

HOW TECHNIQUES, TIPS & TRICKS CHANGE THE COURSE OF DIRECTION IN THE MATCH

The ball came into Ronny's hand from a back pass from fellow team mate center forward who heeded the coach's call to hand the ball to Ronny. Eyes glued on the clock, hearts pounding as sweat poured down his face. Will Ronny live up to the crowd's expectation?

Opponents had banked all hope on Ronny's absence from the game and made good use of the opportunity to tidy up and tie scores at 26/26. Irving, Ronny's coach and confidant of many years frantically moved on the touchline, shouting himself hoarse

"Hand the ball to Ronny," he cried out. Coach Irving had whispered something in Ronny's ears on the reserve bench. That is when Ronny peeled off the sweat shirt pulling it over his head in such haste he tore off the button in the process as he ran down the pitch to stand in line ready to join his team mates in the game.

Ronny got into the action of the game in the dying minutes. Throughout the entire time, he sat on the reserve bench and watched his team mates battle with opponents for the oval ball without saying a word. If you know Ronny, he was aching to go in and do what he does best – make a brilliant run with the ball to touch down.

Coach Irving had reserved Ronny for the countdown in this tournament.

"What is the use?" Sheila, one die hard female fan remarked in mock indignation when Ronny got off the reserve bench and headed for the touchline, skipping rope, his trademark in all games. He always skipped rope prior to going into the game.
However, Sheila's concerns would not alter Coach Irving's decision to field Ronny in the game towards the end.

Modern Jungle Warfare

Modern jungle warfare has highlighted the need for short range detection system capable of "seeing," individual enemy infiltrators concealed in the heavy undergrowth.

Darkness works for the enemy in Vietnam. Guerilla forces, moving quietly at night though the jungle they know so well can neutralize American superiority in weapons with the tactics of surprise. In guarding against such attacks, the Army and the Marine Corps investigated and came up with devices for "illuminating," the defense perimeter at night.

Three field perimeter surveillance radar units have been in used with great success. They all employ pulse Doppler. Target indication is by audio tone – though one of them also used visual scope presentation. The Marines successfully used these devices in Vietnam and elsewhere; but they like the Army are always working to develop superior gear. This innovation was followed by a new generation of field surveillance radar, consisting of three units developed by the Army. All three are lighter, smaller and more versatile than the previous. Display on the new equipment was clearer providing better target definition. How is this information relevant to American

Football? The answer to this question hinges on the topic How Offense can beat Defense in American Football.

The secret behind winning in football game is determined by the amount of time the team puts into plotting to outwit opponents. Muscle power does help a great deal but only as far as it is well coordinated with good strategy does muscle power yield desired outcome in the game.

Battling to blast through the defense 3-4 human wall is daunting without prior proper advance planning of the game. This is where the team benefits from the mathematics of the game. Winning is back to basics on the drawing board.

The team is going against 3-4 front comprising three down linesmen, and four line breakers making up the defense line up. Every day is not Sunday and every game is unique and takes a different shape.

There is no one fit size for all strategy. Be that as it is, running weak side strategy has more appeal and better score results on the list of premium priority strategies in the game. How does it work? This chapter brings you up to date on 3 strategic Tricks and Techniques that Change the Course of Direction in the Match

How Players Move the Ball to Find Opponents End Zone

American football is played between two teams, the offense on the go to move the ball forward into the defense heavily guarded area on full alert. The two teams are separated by the line of scrimmage. Here is a typical line up position of the two teams in the game.

Offense Line Up

Center	Quarter Back	Wide Receiver
Guard	Half Back	Tight End
Defense End	Full Back	

Line of Scrimmage - This is an imaginary line which comes into effect during the game.

Defense Line Up

Nose Tackle	Line Breaker	Corner Back
Defense Tackle	Nickel Back	Safety
Defense End		

The two teams' line ups are maintained throughout the game except when the ball is kicked at the beginning of the game, half time, following a score and in case the ball fails to move forward and cover the ten yard requirement rule. The offense and defense line ups are further broken down to line and backfield. Linesmen in the offense protect the backs men to free them to move the ball down the field.

Positions

Quarter Back – Spearheads the offense. He is also the official ball handler during the game.
1. 5 Offense Linesmen
2. 2 Side Receivers
3. I Running Back
4. 1 Full Back
5. 1 Tight End

Quarter Back

Quarter back is the main man of the match in this squad of five. He is responsible for ball movements with play commencement. He passes the ball off to team mates (Running Back) or throws the ball to one of two receivers. In rare instances, the Quarter Back runs the ball flanked by and guarded by the five linesmen.

Right and Left Tackle

Right and left tackle, guard and center form the formidable force of five that lead the offense to move the ball forward. Running, Full Backs are sometimes referred to as half back, wingback or slot back.

Running Backs

Running backs role include but not exclusive to protecting the quarter back, blocking on run plays and catching the ball in play. Wide receivers are charged with the responsibility of running out in the field of play to catch the ball and block whenever there is need for that action.

Kicking team is required to remain behind the ball at the kick off and isn't allowed to cross the line or advance. Kick off take place in 40 - 70 yard range in the football field. The ball can be also be kicked by a member of the kicking team over a ten yard space to team mate to make a run with it, pass or give it a hard kick aiming at the goal posts. Starting the Game

A coin toss is conducted before the start of football game to determine the team that will have the opening kick. From then on the two opposing teams struggle to possess the ball, which can be achieved in five different ways:

- Turnover on downs – this is when the offensive team fails to move the ball ten yards in 4 downs, thus being inclined to give up the ball to the opposing team.
- Punt – this is when the defensive team prevents the offensive from gaining ten yards in 3 downs, and the ball is punted or free-kicked to the opposing team on 3rd down.
- Safety – this is when the defensive side tackles a player in his own end zone.
- Turnover – this is when a team picks up a ball that has been dropped by the opposing team (fumbling), or blocks a pass thrown by the opposing QB (interception.
- Receiving a kickoff – a kickoff is awarded to the team at the start of every half time and when the opposing team scores.

New Comers to the game

If you are new to the game, the first two situations may not make much sense. The down and distance system is the most confusing concepts in American football. A team is awarded four attempts or downs every time the team takes possession of the ball, to advance it ten yards. Should the team manage to advance the football ten yards or more before the 4 downs are up, they are given four more downs to advance another ten yards, and so forth.

In every segment of the game, the yards gained or lost by each team are determined by the officials, who then place the football where the offense team wound up play. This is at the line of scrimmage.

Line of scrimmage is an imaginary line running across the pitch. This line marks where the offensive team begins every play. A team of officials on the sidelines handle a ten-yard long chain that measures the line of scrimmage every team has to achieve in order to obtain a 1st down. During close plays, the chain can be introduced onto the pitch to calculate the distance between the ten-yard mark and the ball.

End Result

If the team is unable to advance ten yards after 3 downs, it can decide to punt the football to the opposing team, or utilize its 4th down. In the latter, the team has to reach the ten-yard mark, or else give up the ball. When a team decides to punt the ball, it is usually in order to push the opposing team back and give them distance to cover.

However, the other team can decide to return the punt by catching the ball and running back down the pitch. The kicking team hopes to kick the football down the pitch and take down the kick returner of the receiving team before he makes his way down the pitch again.

The ultimate aim in the end is to reach the opponents' goal line. A touchdown is scored when the ball touches the end zone of the opposing team. There are several ways of scoring points in American football in addition to the touchdown.

When a team scores a touchdown, it can decide to pass the ball or run into the end zone to gain a 2-point conversion, or kick a field goal to gain the extra one more point. If a team scores a touchdown or field goal, and attempts the two points or extra point conversion successfully, it is required to kick the football to the other team's side, except in the case of a safety where the scoring team is given the ball on a free kick.

This is referred to as onside kick. However, the ball is considered dead if it is touched by players before the 10 yard space areas of coverage. How does it work?

How Positions Works on Offense Side

Backs strive to move the ball by making a run with it or creating space on the defense line to trap a thrown ball by the quarter back. While the offense works to gain ground and move the ball forward in the game, the defense block any attempt to break through with all it takes within the rules and regulations of the game.

You're wondering what the rest of the team members not mentioned with specific assignment are supposed to be doing during game time. Pattern of play adopted by the team determines the type of play.

This includes all team members at some point or another.

These are the basic assigned roles in the game. No one watches the game with hawk eyes to know the Nickel Back and Defense Tackle haven't been assigned specific roles.

Picture this

The offense is face down and six yards from the quarter backs reach to throw him the ball. The shadow underneath players on bended knees gives poor visibility of the ball.

The defense is on full alert to keep the offense at bay from the end zone, if possible punish them for invading their well guarded territory. In this situation, the defense tactic is to allow the receiver to catch the ball then go for him with hard and forceful attacks forcing offense to the centre to free line breakers. When the offense is finally lined up into one formation, the full back takes liberty to run the weak side and block line breaker.

How Offense Achieves Better Field Position in the Game

The side of the team in possession of the ball is the offense. This makes the other team the defense in the game until they gain control of the ball and vice versa as play moves back and forth. Each team is determined to break the jinx of blockade of the other to advance and score.

10 yards advancement earns the offense points. The offense advances with 4 plays (down) to reach the scoring zone (touchdown and through an awarded free kick aimed to pass the goal line through the two goal posts. 10 yard offense advancement gives the team first, second, third and fourth downs respectively.

If offense is unable to blast through the opponents' human body shield 10 yards in the four downs, the defense gets control of the ball. In American Football lingo, this is referred to as turn over on downs. The meaning of touch down is implied in the action when control of the ball is turned over to the defense.

Touch Down

Excitement in the game is generated when the offense breaks lose to advance the ball to reach the end zone to score 6 points on touchdown. Players also score 3 points on kicking the ball through vertical steel frame goal posts.

Touchdown is rewarded with a two yard line offense advance to score in NFL, 15 yard attempt earn points if the offense converts it gains in one of two ways.

- Kicking the ball through goal posts at 15 yard distance.
- The offense can also choose to re-advance through normal play pattern from the vantage point to gain entrance into the

opponents' end zone.

In either case, the offense has advantage in ball movement within close range to the end zone. That explains why this opportunity earns 1 point from a kick and 2 points for re-advancement moves.

Outwitting the defense through maneuvering runs, passes, following practiced pattern to give one player a clear run with the ball to the end zone are some of the techniques dedicated football players use in the game.

The defense will do anything, attack, push, shove to prevent and fend off the offense from their goal end zone.

Score Difference

If the offense is down 10 points in the game, safety play is the best option out for the simple reason that the team stands the chance to punt the ball. How does the offense achieve field position and ball possession in the game? Here is how better field position pass assist to advance the ball during play.

The offense sensing danger grabs the defender and puts him down. This throws in a gap and opens up the way for the ball carrier to sprint to the end zone from the scrimmage line.

The team could be lucky to get a down. But ideally the team is playing to gain field position in playing to advance the ball in the game. How does the offense gain ball control and possession?

- Two Tricky Techniques Offense uses to Gain Ball Possession Scoring is the ultimate pay back price in the game every dedicated player wants to achieve in the game. The thrill a player feels on touchdown shows all over his face having put the team on the lead with six point touchdown score.

This achievement is satisfying and great but it calls for hard work and collaboration between individual members of the team. Ball advancement to reach the end zone is a challenging task. The offense applies different techniques to gain better field position to achieve this feat.

1. Possession and Ball Passes

Short ball throws of between 8-10 yards are ideal for greater ball control possession. The intention of using the short passes range technique is to put distance between the team and pursuers in the game. This creates room and maintains ball possession in the process.

In the process the team restores the quarter back confidence to have control in the game. The quarter back could also try out for long range throws in addition to short 5 yards distance in which the receiver runs and stops 5 yards up the field then turns back to the quarter back. This strategy is used in the game to gain ball control and better field position. Another way of gaining ball possession is through play action pass.

2. Play Action Pass

"Fake it till you make it," the famed self improvement slogan works wonders in play action pass. This is the quarter back bag of tricks to hand off the ball to running back only to drop back in line and throw the ball at 4 yards distance.

The fake throw trick disorganizes the defense and allows the offense room to penetrate the thick human wall mounted to stop them from gaining entry into the defense end zone area. In addition this trick also gives the quarter back plenty of time and room to throw the ball this time to designated team mate in the field at a calculated long distant range.

The offense follows a specific play pattern to make up a good line of attacks. Defense sole responsibility is to block any attempts by the offense to gain grounds in the game. Defense does not follow a strict pattern of play provided the defense bulwark guard is unshaken to prohibit the offense from the end zone.

How Offense Achieves Better Position

The ultimate goal of American football game is to score. The team needs to advance towards the end zone of the opponent in order to score. There are various strategies that the offense can use to gain yards and subsequently achieve a better position in the field. The three outstanding ones include throwing a field position pass, going for possession pass, and using play action passes to move downfield.

Throwing a Field Position Pass

If the offense is facing 3rd down with more than six yards (3rd and long), the best bet is for the Quarter back QB to throw the ball to a running back beneath the defensive secondary's coverage. In this situation, it is mandatory for the receiver to catch the ball first before the defensive secondary can advance and tackle him.

In the early stages of the game, when the offense is down by 10 or less points, the best bet is to take a safe play on 3rd-and-long, keeping in mind chances of ending up striking the ball are high. In a nutshell, your offense is lifting the white flag and surrendering. This is why passing the ball to the running back is known as a field position pass. The back might get lucky, push through a few tackles, and manage a 1st down, but you are basically playing for field position. It is very unlikely to beat a good defensive team using a 3rd-and-long.

Going for Possession Passes

A possession pass is a short throw of between eight and ten yards, to a tight end or a running back. The aim is not to achieve a 1st down, yet maintain possession of the ball while advancing your yardage in the field. You will often see teams calling possession passes numerous times over a short period in order to help restore the QB's confidence by completing simple passes.

In defensive secondary play away from the scrimmage line, the QB is looking to connect with a wide receiver using a possession pass. The best option is to throw a five-yard hitch. This is where a receiver makes a five yard run up the pitch, halts, and then faces the quarterback.

Using Play Action Passes to move Downfield

A play action pass involves the quarterback faking a pass to a running back, and then dropping back four more yards to throw the ball. By faking the handoff, the defensive backs off, the linebackers hesitate and stop advancing forward once they figure out it is not a running play. This is done in order to retreat and take responsibility of the pass areas. If none of the teams has scored any points, and the offense is on their own twenty-yard line, they can take their chances and throw the ball.

How Defense Beats Offense in the Game

In war, defense is the act of protection from the enemy. Military personnel use heavy artillery to shell the enemy and keep them at a safe distance while strategizing to run them off the ground and out of the place.
In the court of law, the outcome of a case depends on the arguments the defense lawyer lodges in favor of his/her client over the charges.

You wonder why this word is spelt differently yet conveys the same meaning whether in American or British version.

Bottom line, the defense attempts to stop, block the offense from gaining grounds in the game whatever it takes. In NFL nothing short of savage and brutality describes the way players attack and go after each other charging full force like bulls on the loose. Result, the player in possession of the ball is put down "downed."

- **Defense Line Up**

The defense comprise of line backers who will hustle, rush offense players in a bid to gain control of the ball during play time. The main aim is to stop offense running back advance movement on run plays, guard tight end receivers, positioned behind the wall of corner backs in the cover up operation. Deep in the defense line are safeties in the middle of the field behind linebackers who provide "double coverage." This is additional back up force in the defense line.

You're lucky if you leave the pitch without an opponent putting part of your body out of joint in the game. Your head, nose, shoulder protective gear is no match for the incoming force from of offense or defense team member. You get knocked about, so hard your teeth rattles and could fall out.

Woe unto you if you wear false teeth to the game. You wonder if this game is meant for enjoyment or inflicting excruciating pain upon each other. Of course this game would lose its luster without the adrenaline pumping, heart throbbing, dare devil move to break through the opponents blockade even when a player knows the opponents are baying for his blood in attempting to do that.

- **Three Tips of Beating Offense**

In soccer, volley, basket and football games, the ball is the center of attraction. Rules, regulations discussed in chapter two determine the outcome of the game. The different ways and positions the ball is taken in the field during play time also play a role. Offense have immense task of moving the ball forward by runs, kick off and passes and defense are on hand to receive the free kick offs.

Receiving Free Kick Offs

Should the ball travel on air untouched by any player to the end, the result is touchback. In touch back, the ball is placed at 20 yard line on the receiving team's side to resume and continue play. The starting point in this case is also known as line of scrimmage in ball kick off during play in which the ball floats untouched to the receiving team end zone.

Kick off that goes astray and out of bounds at any point in the file and not end zone without the receiving team touching the ball is illegal kick off. This calls for a kick at 5 yards distance closer to the kicking team's goal line. In chapter ten you read details of out of bounds ball.

Downed Player

If a player is downed and the ball comes to rest in the process, it is termed dead. In this case, game officials take appropriate next appropriate action to spot the ball where the player carrying the ball was downed. This point marks the beginning place for ball play in the next segment of play in the continuation of the game. This is point is referred to as line of scrimmage in American Football.

Defense will "down," offense player by taking him down from whichever direction front, back or sideway.

- The player feels hands shredding him to pieces if he holds onto the ball. The best bet is to throw the ball to a team mate. That will take attention off the player as the opponents follow ball movement.
- Pushing, shoving, sliding, "Get him down," shouts ring out from fans and coach. The ball is the center of action and attention. The ball has to be kept in play all the time. Attempts to stop the ball from moving forward, backward is not part of the game plan.
- NFL has perimeters earmarked for play. Players risk penalty going off the line of demarcation on the field. Keep playing with eyes wide open.

NFL players get away with murder in the field. If you drive opponent backwards instead of going for the ball, the player is awarded with a penalty kick off taken from the point you stopped him dead on the tracks wrongfully.

How an Offense Can Beat a Defense

The defense setup is one of the most significant considerations in football a coach takes seriously to determine what plays to call and which offense to run. There are different strategies for beating different defenses.

1. Fighting a 3 – 4 front

The 3-4 fronts have 4 linebackers and 3 down linemen. In facing such a setup, the best strategy for the offense is to run away from the difficult end or to the weak side. The weak side lead is one of the running plays he can adopt. In this tactic, the DE (defense end) tries to control and push the LT (offensive tackle) inside towards the middle of the line to leave the OLB in charge of plenty of open area to defend.

The offense assumes the I formation, with the fullback running to the weak side to block the linebacker by shoving him to the inside. The LOT (left offensive tackle) lets the defensive end push him slightly; manipulates the defender into thinking that he is in control of the play. This is a ploy to allow the offensive lineman grab the defender, withholding him and moving him to the right and out of the way. This provided a clear running lane for the ball carrier after hitting the line of scrimmage.

2. Battling a 4-3 front

There are several ways an offense can beat a 4-3 front of 3 linebackers and 4 down linemen. However, the most common strategy is attack referred to as the bubble side (where the 2 linebackers of the defensive side are located). It involves the RG (right guard) blocking down the N (nose tackle), with the fullback running into the hole and blocking the ILB (front side linebacker).

The DE (defensive end) is blocked by the RT (right tackle), preventing him from reaching the middle, while the OLB (outside linebacker) is blocked and contained by the TE (tight end). Once the ball carrier makes his way to the line of scrimmage, there should be an open space between the right tackle and right guard of the offense.

3. Beating the 4 Across Defense

This type of defense involves playing all 4 secondary players about twelve yards away from the line of scrimmage. The offense needs to have 2 WR (wide receivers) run comeback routes, with the TE (tight end) running a sixteen yard in route and the two RBs swinging out to the left and right, in order to beat this defense. If the defense senses that the QB intends to throw the ball to the WR on the left and decides to send a linebacker to intercept, the QB can pass to the running back instead, since he will not be covered. If the reverse happens, the quarterback can throw to the wide receiver.

4. Battling Press Coverage

This is when the two cornerbacks of the defense team are on the line of scrimmage, marking the outside receivers closely. One strategy of beating this defense is to pass the ball to the TE (tight end), who then makes a run to the center of the pitch. Another alternative is to pass to the RB (running back) who is swinging out towards the left side. The WR (wide receivers) that are being pressed take off in the opposite direction to make a clear run with the ball.

5. Fighting through a zone coverage

In the zone coverage, the cornerbacks are not in press coverage, which means that they're playing away from the line of scrimmage. The curl is the best strategy against a defense employing zone coverage, and the most efficient time to utilize it is on 1st-and-ten. This involves a WR (wide receiver) running ten to twelve yards, and simply curling or hooking back towards the QB (quarterback).

6. Choosing an offense against a zone blitz

If the defense tends to blitz a lot from the corner (safeties or linebackers coming from both wide sides of the line of scrimmage to counter your offensive tackles), the best bet for the offense is to line up with 2 tight ends to aid pass-protect. The offense needs to find the weakest defender of the opposing team in order to overcome a zone blitz using a passing attack (be it a linebacker, safety, or cornerback). The quarter should then throw the ball to the opposite side of the defense with more players. For instance, if there are 4 defensive players to the left of the quarterback, he should punt the ball to his right. However, the offense should also protect the side that is being attacked by the defense.

At the height of football is Super Bowl; the world's most watched live TV program with over 100 million viewers in the US alone. That probably explains why 30 second commercials for the last Super Bowl cost as high as $4 million. If you have been thinking that Super Bowl is not as popular as some people tend to say it is, checkout this

"http://www.sportingcharts.com/articles/nfl/how-many-people-watch-the-super-bowl-each-year.aspx"

these stats will prove you otherwise. But stats will probably not give you the much needed thrill for the game. In the next chapter, we will highlight some of the most popular matches.

Tricks & Techniques Of Football Secondary Team

Whenever defensive backs take position to be part of a football secondary team, they hardly know if the play will be a run or a pass. In a flash, once the ball has been snapped, they must determine the intentions of the offense. In order to figure out the offense's plans, the defensive backs have to use certain tricks and techniques.

- **Performing a Bump & Run**

The idea here is to get in the receivers' faces and jam them or chuck them with both hands as they approach from the scrimmage line. The ultimate goal is to hit the receiver in the chest and interfere with the timing of the pass play, subsequently forcing him to take a bad leap.

Usually, the receiver is pushed by the defensive back in order to influence his direction. A defensive back has a general idea of which way the receiver intends to go. The defense forces the receiver to adjust his pass route by bumping the receiver to one side. Defensive backs are very careful with the bump & run: it is legal to hit the receivers five yards within the scrimmage line. However, hitting the receivers beyond that will result in a penalty. In some cases, you might notice the defensive backs hitting the receivers beyond the five yards. In this case, the officials might or might not catch them.

- **Hanging on to a Receiver**

When a defensive back has bumped or attempted to jam a receiver, they have to be able to adjust their position and stay with the running receiver. In some cases, the defensive back, particularly a cornerback, could wind up chasing after the receiver. The defensive back can turn by making half turns and rotating the upper body towards the receiver's side.

A defensive back is required to train his footwork in order to be able to take long strides while running back from the scrimmage line and covering a receiver. He should also be able to perform a long crossover step using his feet while maintaining an erect upper body position. This can be a difficult technique to achieve, since the defensive back is required to move backwards at the same speed with which the receiver is running forward.

- **Stemming Around**

Stemming refers to the action defensive backs make when they are moving around having settled down in positions prior to the snap of the football by the offense. Stemming is designed to fool the offense's quarterback into making a poor decision where the ball would be directed. The defensive football embraces this tactic more and more to create doubt in the QB's mind, thereby interfering with his decision-making.

Summary

Chapter five focuses on three areas of the game prone to produce tangible result in the end. The three areas include but exclusive to tricks and techniques players use to move the ball with the aim of finding opponents end zone. Second, the chapter points out two different tricks offense apply to achieve better field position. Third, this chapter shows you six tips of beating defense by the offense and concludes with tricks and techniques of football secondary team.

Chapter Six

HOW INDIVIDUAL PLAYER'S ATTITUDE INFLUENCE OUTCOME OF THE GAME

If you're fascinated by track and field events, no doubt you enjoy relay race. The four member team runs the best time, hands over the baton to the finished line to claim victory. Individual players in football game work extremely hard and consistently together during the game. In some cases, the brilliant performance of individual player carries the day but it is the outcome of the game that counts the most.

Football teams have played the game one man down to the end when a member of the team is ejected for failing to obey the set rules. In some cases the team with one man deficit weathers the storms of pressure from opponents to run the full time in the game and win. But such cases are rare.

Playing football with ten man squad instead of eleven has great disadvantages. It puts a lot of pressure on the remaining team members. A chance of winning the game is such a situation is difficult but not impossible.

Time is another factor which could influence the outcome of the game in this scenario. The team member ejected from the game at the end of the fourth quarter is not as pronounced as playing with one man down in the three quarters of the game.

Imagine running this race in a team of 3 against 4 member team opponents. Only a miracle make the three man team clinch the title in this race. The trio is no match for the quartet in this run.

"An individual remains an individual, not only from birth to death, but actually long before birth until long, after death," Joel Goldsmith wrote in his book "The Infinite Way." You can learn five lessons from this statement. The five include perfection, potential, participation, pitfall and practices.

Five Lessons from Individual Football Player

1. Perfection is Ultimate

You're created perfect in every way. Thinking otherwise won't change the fact. You're endowed with 100% brain power as anyone else. You've sound physical body capable of doing things beyond your wildest of dreams. Now you know why individuals excel in different tasks and undertakings.

You've the same ability within waiting to be tapped. You may not necessarily ascribe to the teachings of the Bible but you can borrow a leaf from the words of wisdom in this book from time to time.

"I am fearfully and wonderfully made...,"the psalmist wrote. If you turn back to Genesis account of creation 2:7,

"Let us make man in our image, after our likeness..," the Bible says. If you're not perfect, so is God. If the thought of God sounds distant, think of your own parents. What do you think of your parents, perfect or imperfect? Tie this proposition with your own ability. You have insatiable urge go excel in the game of football because you've what it takes to play the game. You're in the game to win not lose. If you doubt this assurance here is a little exercise to help you visualize winning the match clearly.

You don't doubt the image on the opposite side of the mirror is you. But it goes deeper than that. Standing in front a mirror is one thing, approving or disapproving the image starring back at you is another. What counts is the outcome. The same is true in the game of football. If you have poor self image and losing in the game looms large in your mind that is the outcome you program the mind to get.

On the other hand if you go out set to win, you've a head start in the game. The body will cooperate with the mind and together you've a formidable force. If all individual team members share the same passion to win, you enjoy the game of football knowing winning is within reach.

2. Potential Within has the Promise

How do you identify and unleash the potential within in the game of football? You've success stories of champions in the game and want more than anything else in the world to be counted one of them.

Six Steps to Unleash Individual Potential in Football Game

Here are six steps to guide individual players determine the potential within.

- **Highlight the qualities you consider favour your success in this game**

    o   Remind yourself of the task at hand.
    o   Retrace your tracks to budget time.
    o   Refresh the mind with positive images of success from

the video clips of the game, the motivation talk, pin up photos of your heroes in the game on the wall in your room at home, locker in school.

- **Hold on to the End**

This move will assist you and quicken your pace in the game. You end up liberating yourself from unwanted baggage and functioning fully in support of the team to win by identifying your particular place in the team. Every team member has a specific task in the game to move the ball forward, backward. Identify your position in the team and hold on because winning depends on it.

- **Have it Your Way**

You've been practising with the team and pretty much know the moves to keep the ball in motion and moving towards the opponents end zone. The moment you've been waiting for has come. What more could you ask for? It is do or die. Your best shot on the game depends on the moment.

Forget about everything else including the row you had with team mate in the locker room. Now is the time for individual as well as collective action and your contribution is crucial to lifting the super bowl trophy. You can't afford to squander this opportunity by letting your mind stray off from the pitch and action in the game. A similar opportunity isn't going to come by way in life like this again.

- **Hang in There**

You're capable of scoring the big win with touchdown; kick off the ball for a 3 point lead in the game of football. You've the potential within to be the man of the moment in the match. No standards are set in the game to bar teams from winning. The rules and regulations are reasonable, fairly simple and straight forward.

Ronny, the small town football player made history by looking within self to unleash his potential in the game. Ronny's name does not come up in who is who records of football game but his action speaks volumes as an outstanding football player in a class of his own. He lifted off the lid of limitation out of his life to achieve this feat. Try it out. It really does work. If you've difficulty getting a grip in the game and yet love it, liaise with other team members and the coach

- **Harmony in the Game**

What constitutes good team work? Teamwork in the game of football is similar to taking part in relay race. Individual players of the team work forge a united front to counter the defence or offense. You're expected to play your part by putting in 100% contribution in the team. Winning the match depends on consistency and cohesiveness of the team. In some cases, quality performance of the team is not so much prior knowledge of what is expected but the hidden potential to rise to the occasion in the event. You alone determine your lassitude.

- **Help Yourself Learn Lassitude.**

You would rather spend time playing football than bouncing basketball on the concrete field. You draw satisfaction running around chasing the oval ball, working on strategies for touchdown with teammates.

"Successful team work is Unity in Diversity." Your individual contribution determines the outcome in the game. You know what you're capable of doing, the weakness and and strengths, favourite and not so favourite moves in the game. Use the strengths as stepping stones to improve quality performance in the game. You can unleash your potential if you learn your lassitude. No matter how you feel, don't let your weaknesses blur your vision of winning the game. You can.

3. Practices to Steer Success

Chapter four focuses on five strategies that make winning football game a reality and not a dream. Practice tops this list of strategies. Make time to understand the techniques, tips and tricks of football outlined in chapter five to lay strategies in the game. These are your arsenals for playing the game.

Practice to perfect them through, re-examination, review, reason, and role each contributes to winning. Focus on the outcome as you practice. Think of the real game and the practice as a dress rehearsal. This is your clarion call to unravel pitfalls in football game.

4. Participation in the Game

Real change starts in the mind. This is the turnaround action from heading in one direction to a different direction in life. Change of mind brings lasting solutions to the challenges you face in the game. Take a look at Seven Ways of Making the Most of Individual Participation in the Game

Seven Ways of Making the Most of Individual Participation in the Game

• Re-examination.

Your commitment to re-examine the purpose of playing the game paves the way for better individual collective participation in the match. This calls for change of mind.

You want to succeed at scoring touchdown. Switch the mind to focus on that outcome in the game. If you're daunted by failure to make it stick, substitute it with fulfillment. Realize playing football in high school, college is typical of super bowl game. It is all in the mind.

- **Realization.**

No point waiting until you're selected in the team to take part in the super bowl game. Do it now, today in high school, college football game participation. Participation assists you to develop new perception of the big game.

 o Perspective

You've access to video clips, photos of the game. You also have a chance to watch others play at a higher level on television, read newspaper sports report on the game. You've ton of information online on the game if you want to improve. Not to mention your active participation in high school, college football team. In reality, there is difference between high school, college football and the super bowl. The rules and regulations are the same.

 o Perfection

You reach out for pain killers if you've a headache. If the pain persists you seek medical advice. That's the pattern in relieving pain. Perfecting performance in football game is much the same. You're playing high school, college today; tomorrow you're a member of one of the two teams competing in super bowl tournament. It costs nothing to visualize and bring the big game into focus now to perfect your performance.

- **Review Super Bowl Game as typical of any Football Match.**

You preview pictures and documents to select what you need to use in the computer. Your preview of the real game has the same effect. The biblical narrative of Christ's transfiguration best illustrates this point.

In this narrative, future events were manifested in advance according to the gospel of Mathew 17: 1-13. This incident foreshadows future events in God's plan of action for salvation for mankind. Use the same strategy to review football game at any level to get a foretaste of the big game in sharp focus.

- **Reasoning through Questioning**

Your inner voice is a constant irritation that won't go away. This nagging of inner voice to become the next football champion won't cease until you take action and steps to follow your heart desires. You create your own world with unlimited opportunities in all fields including playing football. Reason; ask questions to gauge your level of competence in preparation for the game. You can't do better than that.

- Role Models

A child learns on his/her own. No amount of handholding, hustling harnesses knowledge and skills imparted by parents; teachers to ensure the child takes that information in equal measure. It's up to the child. Life presents lots of instructions for the adult learner. You're your own best instructor and role model for the child within you. You're grown up in body size shape and stature, but you'll never outgrow the child within you. You can become as good as if not better than your role model in the game.

"It is the child in man that is the source of …uniqueness and creativeness, and the playground…for the unfolding of his capacities and talents," Eric Hoffer observed.

- **Reach out**.

You're determined to become the next football champion in season. Great! It's the only passage way to play in the super bowl game. You've been practicing. The real game is here at last. No postponement. No matter how ill prepared you're. You only have one choice, reach out and grab this opportunity of a lifetime.

- **Remember**

School, college, local team football is a link in the chain of participation for the real game.

5. Pitfalls in Participation in Football Game

"Nothing much happens on Fridays," one local daily newspaper weekend diary edition comments on university students life. Weekend schedule gives room for social life. Players have similar behavioral patterns. You're done with practice but not peer group pressure. Three pitfalls stare football players on the face. Search for identity, social mirror and success image. Left unchecked, these three pitfalls could ruin a promising career in football game.

Players are under enormous pressure from all sides, the economy, the contemporary success image and the social mirror. The effects of these three are the main pressure points in pursuing academic excellence in education.

- **Search for Identity**

"Who am I?" This is the first of four fundamental basic life questions, anyone keen on success in life needs to address. No one can answer this question adequately for you. Your heart desire to participate in the game prompts you to identify with likeminded persons. However, it is more than partnering with others it is tied down to purpose. What is your purpose for participating in this game, excitement, exercise, economic value?

- **Social Mirror**

Football teams are like institutions. Institution outlive individual in life. You join Patriots, Seattle Seahawks, and Denver Broncos among other football teams that have been in existence for years. The founders and are no longer members of the team. These folks ran a rood race having set up the team from scratch to set standards you go in to match or break to maintain the original team spirit.

Spectators, coaches, fans have great expectations on the team's performance at the national league. It is against that social mirror your participation in the game is gauged. Society standards are governed by culture. Football is a way of life sports in America. This sporting event forms part of American culture.

- **Society Effect**

How does society view failures in this game? Take a look at the commercials. Individual football players are portrayed as role models in society. How do you view the players? No any different from the rest of society members. You darn well know the pressure of making it big in the big league. That is the reason you need to weigh your options and strike a balance in taking part in this game. .

Don't let the pitfalls stand in the way of becoming the champion you always dreamed of in football. No pressure from any quarters is too great for you to overcome if you want and choose. It's Your Call

Unraveling pitfalls in football game depend on search for identify, social mirror and the effect these bring to bear on society. These are three pitfalls only cover a small spectrum of a player's life. There are many other pitfalls depending on individual situation. No matter the kind, no matter the magnitude of pitfalls and challenges the individual encounters, the final say to attain the ultimate goal in playing football rests you always. .No one knows you better than you do. It's up to you to walk the tight rope in the game to the finish line.

Imagine your life ten, twenty years from now. How different will your life in the field of football be? Focus on that picture as you practice to play the next game. It's the only picture that's worth hanging on the wall of your heart.

Chapter Seven

HOW DIFFERENT PAST SUPER BOWL CHAMPIONS WERE WON

Super Bowl attracts large audiences to stadiums, television and radio broadcasting stations. The popularity of this game makes it one of the leading grossing sports from commercials, gate collections and selling of insignia, food, drinks, gambling as well as on spot thrills of the game by players and spectators on the pitch.

You're unable to make the trip and attend the live event in person. You've access to the game on television screen live on world class sporting stations. Super Sports, Gillette World of Sports lead the pack of world class stations including news bulletin update report on sporting events.

How the Patriots Won the 2015 Super Bowl

"The best way to motivate people is to put them against one another..." This quote from Thomas J. Watson, Jr. former IBM CEO observed. However, in the 2015 Super Bowl tournament this observation had a positive ring to it although in most cases it is counterproductive in organization life cycle. 3

Seattle Seahawks were down by 4 points during the one minute playtime remaining in the game. Only a miracle could change the course of direction in this game because the odds and time were against Seattle Seahawks team.

Loss loomed large in the eyes of spectators but Seattle Seahawk players showed no sign of surrender. The team would only concede defeat at the blow of the last whistle in the game. If you think motivation is just another English language catch phrase you would think twice when you read how the twist of events influenced the outcome of 2014 Super Bowl tournament competition. Seattle Seahawk players were not simply motivated to play on; this team demonstrated that indeed motivation is motive in action during this game.

Any attempt in the dying minutes of the game provided a lifeline to the team and in the end Patriots led with 28-24 win in the 2015 Super Bowl tournament.

- Here are the highlights of events which changed the course of the game

Seconds ticked away as Jermaine Kearse caught the ball mid air going down inside the 10 yard line. This was rare breakthrough opportunity the team could us to improve their chance of winning the game. However, anticipation was thwarted by Malcolm Butler's quick action. Butler stepped inside the goal line to pick up the ball.

The Patriots were trailing Seattle Seahawks by 10 points in the game. Tom Brandy revived the spirit of New England Patriots team with two touchdowns in the eight minute to put the team back on course and on the lead in the second quarter of the game.

The two teams were running neck to neck at half time break. Seattle Seahawks regained composure and control of the game in the third quarter. The big throws by Wilson and outstanding run by Lynch gave the Seahawks 155 yards advance in the game. Wilson scored on his third run attempt late in the third quarter.

The heat after a scoreless first quarter had given the two teams steam to go all out. The Patriots scored first to leading with short passes to advance 65-70 yards towards the opponents' end zone. Brandy was the man of the match in this game. He engineered Brandon LaFell 11 yard touchdown.

Along pass from Wilson to Christ Mathews gave the Seahawks back a lifeline in the second quarter of the game and Marshwan Lynch put together 3 excellent plays to tidy up and bring the game to a tie at 7. The big breakthrough came in the last 2 seconds of the game when Wilson and Mathews teamed up to wrap up the game.

In the last minute of the game, Brandy hooked up with Julien Edelman for a 3 yard touchdown to seal the Patriots clear lead. Although the Seahawks were the favorites with Marshwan Lynch dominating the game in the second half, New England Patriots team pulled from behind and won the 2015 Super Bowl game 28-24.

How the Seahawks Won 2014 Super Bowl XLVIII

New York – Seattle Seahawk brilliant performance in Super Bowl XLVIII handed Denver Broncos a humiliating 43-8 deserved defeat. This game marked the greatest margin score win in the history of American Foot ball in over two decades. It was watched by 111.5 million fans and supporters across Fox Television networks.

The Seahawks won the Super Bowl for the first time after thrashing the Broncos forty three – eight, under Coach Pete Carroll. With the aid of GM John Schneider, the coach had spent the last 4 years building the deepest, toughest, and most flexible defense in football.

The biggest stage of the game provided them with the opportunity to display the success of their vision to the world. The weather could have been a hindrance factor in the 1[st]Northeast outdoor Super Bowl.

However, The Broncos and Peyton Manning received perfect conditions – forty nine degrees at kickoff – the only challenge being the worst possible opponents.

A number of specific highlights in the game are worth noting. In addition to interests, this is the first ever in and outdoor, cold weather game played in the history of Super Bowl. The media had a field day. Live coverage rating recorded between 44.5/70 making Super Bowl the highest ranking sporting event of the year.

The ratings of this tournament continued to rise through the four quarter segment play periods in this tournament. This event dwarfs music diva Beyonce and Madonna viewership of 110.8 million and 114.0 million respectively two years prior.

Live coverage in the US was extended to Spanish language Fox channel and digital platforms for the first time. Streams average reached 523,000 viewers. How did the Seattle Seahawks do it?

This Super Bowl XLVIII has not been billed the biggest night of Fox Prime time in history for nothing. It started with pre-game shows watched by 23.1 million viewers and peaked at 31.1 viewers which translated into 68.4 viewers on kick offs.

The main event was featured on Fox 7.00-11.00 Prime Time and it attracted 96.4 million viewers. This is a huge jump in the number of people glued on the edge of their seats biting finger nails with eyes riveted on television screens watching Super Bowl one of top seven popular games in the United States of America. These figures only Fox television network coverage, NBC and other channels are unaccounted for in these statistics. In the great moment of the game, viewers were treated to Percy's memorable touchdown score kick off, Malcolm Smith's ball interception for return touchdown plus many more outstanding brilliant performances by the Seahawks in the game.

Denver Broncos had stunning performance setting NFL record on scores during regular season. Players and spectators expected repeat performance by the team during Super Bowl. Denver Broncos hopes were dashed when Seattle Seahawks thrashed the team 43-8 during the 2014 Super Bowl match.

Seattle Seahawks performance carried the day when this team humiliated Denver Bronco opponents before a capacity crowd of fans and enthusiasts. The Seahawks pushed and punished Denver Broncos into 4 turnovers. Denver Bronco that set the NFL standard in the season was no match for the marauding Seattle Seahawks in this game. Mistakes are costly. Denver Broncos snap gave way to safety play marking the beginning of the end of hope for the team which was touted to win this match.

The Seahawks capitalized on Denver Broncos snap mistake and responded with ferocious agility to drive the opponents' hard taking 8-0 point lead. Percy Harvin's set up the pace with a 30 yards run on reverse. Despite his dismal performance during off season while nursing a hip injury he made a startling run in this game.
A pass from Manning through Demaryien Thomas landed on Seattle Seahawks hands and led to the first touchdown of the game. Marshwan Lynch put the Seahawks to 15-0 lead with one yard score. The defense was out of position and place.

Manning could have done the touchdown without quarter back Russell's assistance who rubbed more salt on Denver Broncos injury in the tournament with 18-25 for 206 yards two touchdowns.

However, Denver Bronco team was not about to give up before the game is over. The team attempted come back in the second quarter pounding down Seattle Seahawks defense territory. But the damage had been done. Denver Broncos efforts didn't yield any tangible fruits in the quarter. Malcolm Smith picked up the ball deflected from Manning and ran the 69 yards stretch for a touchdown that sealed the Seattle Seahawks lead at 22-0.

This wasn't Denver Broncos day at the pitch. Any attempt at come back to shine was met with disappointment resulting from one mistake after another which cost the team dearly in the end. Manning and Thomas collaborated to widen the Seahawks 30-0 lead in the third quarter of the game with a touchdown when Wilson found Jermaine Kearse for a 23 yard touchdown from ball fumble by the Broncos.

Thomas wrapped up the Broncos defeat with 14 yard touchdown pass from Manning. Baldwin delivered the touchdown in the fourth quarter which sent Denver Broncos parking. There was no more Denver Broncos could do except to concede humiliating defeat and plan for next season's comeback. Would they have a chance after the 43-8 defeat by Seattle Seahawks?

Twists and Turns in the Game

Denver's offense was pushed around by Seattle at each level of the defense. Denver's tackles were consistently overcome by pass rushers Cliff Avril and Chris Clemons, making Manning rather uncomfortable. When the time came for Manning to throw, there were no receivers to open quickly. Kam Chancellor (Safety) made a couple of significant hits and found Manning to set the tone of the game. Byron Maxwell and Richard Sherman did an outstanding job against the outside receivers of Denver. Linebackers Bobby Wagner and K.J. Wright were all over the pitch.

The team was excellent at every little thing. They could hit, didn't allow yardage after the catch, and had the ability to force game-determining turnovers, such as the sixty nine yard pick six by Smith. Manning was inclined to move in pocket during almost every single throw, while the counterpart's running game was thwarted. It was a struggle to complete every 1st down.

Russell Wilson did his best on 3rd downs, but the defense of Seahawks team was basically an afterthought for the better part of the game. Percy Harvin made the score 29-0 after returning a kickoff for a touchdown, at which point the Seahawk's offense had thirteen points only, seven of these coming on a short pitch after a turnover. The events of the night seemed almost hard to believe – the Bronco's offense, which appeared to be efficient throughout the season, seem completely dazed. They had not prepared for the moment. It was time for the Seahawks to shine. The team, which was constructed from scratch, had been waiting for this game for 4 seasons. Today, it still holds its reputation for having one of the best defenses in the history of NFL.

Three Outstanding Super Bowl XLIX Plays

There are 3 plays that stand out in Super Bowl XLIX as critical to the victory of the Patriots against the Seahawks.

1. The 21 reception of Julian Edelman

The Patriots' 3 drives in the 3rd quarter, after they fell behind, twenty four – fourteen, was made up of 6, 5 and 4 plays, with the last one stretching into the 4th quarter by 2 plays.

The team faced 3rd and fourteen on their first real possession of the 4th quarter. However, Tom Brady came up and threw a punt to Julian Edelman over the center for twenty one yards to keep their hopes up and pull the team to midfield. This was a midst the resistance of Kam Chacellor, the excellent safety of the Seahawks, who gave Edelman a quivering hit at the NE 49.

After 6 plays, the Patriots had reached the end zone after a Danny Amendola and Brady connection, and the Seahawks' lead had been reduced to 24 – 21.

2. The touchdown reception of Julian Edelman

Football game winning touchdown is the most significant play of any game. However, how the play pans out in the game is the bonus significance. Edelman ran the same route that almost led to a touchdown for New England during a previous possession. He cut towards the center of the end zone while aligned on Brady's left, and then rapidly reversed his course, before fading back to the sideline. Tharold Simon, Edelman's defender, was beaten, in the same way that he previously was when the pass slipped off Julian's fingertips. This made the touchdown reception almost too easy.

3. The tackle of Don't'a Hightower against Marshawn Lynch

On the second last play of the Seahawks, Marshawn Lynch, the star running back, was brought to a halt just before reaching the goal line, with Don't'a Hightower, the Patriots' linebacker, making the crucial tackle. He did this by getting hold of Lynch's feet, before Akeem Ayers drove him to the ground.

American Football is Big Business

American Football is big business in the United States of America. It is not simply bigger or more business inclined than the English Premier Football League. But football in United States is different. The term big business traces its meaning to American Skyscrapers and Conglomerates origin. The size and structure of United States with diverse cultural heritage, favors large scale business interests in pursuit of happiness and self interest.

"Business men who do not know how to fight worry and die young," World-famous Dr. Alexis Carrel says.

American magnate on his yacht in the high seas, private jumbo jets flying across continents with a handful crew, the images, territories of American business are defined in literature, legend and living sound. The same is true with big business image in American football. American football game without spectators cheering is not a game. However, if you're unable to attend the super bowl, you don't miss much watching the game on television.

- **How American Football Represents Business Interests**

The importance of Big Business in American life is evident in American football. It is different. It has style, strategy and it satisfies spectators, players, and the American economy.

United States is a country known for celebrities and millionaires. Where in the world do you find big cars, big houses, and big sports stadiums than in United States? America is the 20th century industrial power from big business and American football is one of them. Big business in America is fascinating, yet it is moderately fair and economically viable. It is an essential part of the way America functions internally, and that functioning is spread and maintained in every sphere of American life, including sporting events such as football.

What difference does it make sitting in the grandstand watching American football?

Many spectators think of the grandstand as an entitlement. However, and with all due respect to celebrities and VIPs entitlement is not the same as benefits in the game. There is little doubt that the excitement in the game is the same across board whether you're watching the game from the grandstand in the middle or anywhere in the stadium. The greater space and quite of the grandstand is necessary for hard pressed spectators to mix and mingle with the rest of the crowd in cheering the favorite team to victory. If you need to work and watch the game at the same time, you can. If you need comfort and rest you've got it covered in the grand stand. On top of that grand stand ticket carries with it tangible proof of the game's faith in the spectator.

All over the world, grandstands are revered as the finest place to watch games. When you want to sell a product in the market place, you must believe in it. It shows that you appreciate quality. That is what separates grandstands from the rest of football stadium.

o **Media Frenzy**

Media sells audience to advertisers. Much of entertainment content on television serve the purpose of attracting stereotype target audiences, and is dependent on advertisement for survival. The viewer is bombarded with advertisements before, in between and at the end of the game.

o **Workplace**

In the manufacturing industry, products would come through the assembly line without team work. Employees are given specific tasks to perform. These tasks are assigned to individuals in the respective departments. Departmental heads supervise those under their charge to make sure for example that the flour for baking bread is ordered on time in adequate quantity.

Those who run the oven do not double up as sweepers of factory floors. Office staff deals with correspondence. The bakery is run on a chain of command to get the bread you need for bread fast ready the next morning fresh and sweet.

Marketing and sales department have specific assignments. You don't realize how many people worked behind the scene to produce the bread you eat for breakfast in the morning at home. The pieces of bread are produced through team work by many sweating the small stuff.

Summary

This chapter features two recent outstanding super bowls game wins of 2014 and 2015 respectively. Seattle Seahawks brilliant performance during 2014 Super Bowl game is a milestone in the history of super bowl league. Although Denver Bronco team was humiliated by paying dearly for the mistakes in this seasonal tournament, the team kept sportsman spirit to play the full period without carving under pressure of the eminent loss in the game.

You can draw a number of lessons from both teams to improve on individual tasks and challenges in life. Three outstanding Super Bowl XLIX plays feature prominently in this chapter. These two tournaments also bring out the best of American big business in the game of football.

Chapter Eight

HOW OTHER INDIVIDUALS CONTRIBUTE TO THE SUCCESS OF THE GAME

There is nothing, (well, almost nothing), quite as good as watching American football live. It gives newspapers, something else to write about besides politics and the games politicians play. Football wakes up sleepy shareholders of the team.

Back to Football Boardroom Basics

The fracas in the field, starring two rival teams in the eye may not be classic in comparison to the super bowl game loss on the coach. However, it involves intrigues, twists and turns that make the game of football worth watching. Here are ten survival strategies the coach needs to maintain his position in the team and lead the side to victory in the season.

Ten Survival Strategies for the Coach

Flatter the players, don't talk unless you have to, arrange out of field meetings with superiors whenever you're about to make an important decision (so that no one can blame you if things go wrong) and never offer to resign when the team loses because there is always a chance that your resignation will be readily accepted.

This formula is guaranteed to get the coach by and over the top of challenges in his line of duty. But in a tough highly contested Super Bowl tournament, the coach needs a handful tactics to hang on to his job. Here are the 10 strategies.

1. Don't be A Big Bully

This is an elementary precaution, but its remarkable how many intelligent people including football coaches ignore it. Life is much safer below the top. Humor the players. Give the players a chance to air their views and not boss the meeting all through. Choose a place well away from the usual surrounding to meet your superiors.

2. Trust Your Instincts

The so sincere superiors with firm handshakes and a barrage of phony compliments are far more dangerous than the shifty, insecure players. Straight eye looking is designed to lull you into false sense of security – to reveal inconsistencies in your leadership ability. Don't get duped.

3. Swim with the Current

Superiors don't take kindly to people who challenge their opinions without good reason. If the top man in the team draws you into an argument, it's good not to say too much. Buy time if need be and in the end yield with a yes answer to appease his blotted ego in the meeting.

"If there is any one secret of success, it lies in the ability to get the other person's point of view and see things from that person's angle as well as our own." Henry Ford said.

4. Smart Alex posses Threat

Most teams are owned by people who have long passed their Level of Incompetence in the game. This lot surround themselves with even lower grade individuals in order to make their survival stay. Clever coaches represent an obvious threat. Try to blend in; answer a difficult question with another and resist the temptation to point out that a colleague, superior, is talking nonsense during board meetings.

5. Make Champions

In politics everyone tries to pick a potential winner to run with; there is no better way to fame than choosing the right person for support. The same is true in business and football. The coach stands at the crossroads to choose the player of the moment and make him feel that he can count on his support. If you are right (which is not always guaranteed he will not forget your help in years to come if he is appointed to board membership of the team or scale up the ladder of success in the league.

6. Forge Alliances

It is always good to have friends in high places and successful coaches devote much time and attention to the pursuit of useful contacts. When the team runs into trouble, it's these friends you can turn to lift you up. So it makes good sense to entertain managers of insurance, football equipment manufacturers,' merchant bankers, Bank Governors and anyone who might come in handy when the going gets tough in the field of football.

7. Be Happy Someone Appreciates

You've assisted a colleague up the ladder of success; don't expect a pat on the back or gratitude for the good job. If you think he can't wait to repay you, you're in for a rude shock. He probably can't wait to get past you. In the meantime he will resent being forever indebted to you if you persist on bringing up the issue in conversations.

8. Know the Value of Pessimism

Try forecasting the wins and gains of the team. The actual deficit could be less with couple million dollars in gate collections but you will be hailed as a genius. This familiar ploy works remarkably well many times. Make an optimistic forecast and you risk trouble. If it proves right no one will praise you for making good your promise.
Be pessimistic and stake holders will be delighted that you have managed to beat your own prediction. The figures may still be a

disaster by any normal reckoning but it shouldn't' be difficult to convince people up high in the hierarchy of the team that others are to blame and that the outcome of the game could have been worse if not for your impressive managerial talents.

9. Be a Good Window Dresser

A coach needs to know how to juggle the various elements that go into making the team. It may involve pumping up stock in business for example, delaying payment for goods delivered which you have authority to sign for. The main purpose is to get past the annual meeting and to be safe for another year in the job. Most company results are not merely out of date, yet bear no slightest relationship to the trend of monthly figures.

10. Study Survival Tactics

There are countless people in the manufacturing industry, as in politics and sports that prosper despite their obvious incompetence. They are the professional survivors, the people who devote their days to business of manufacturing and selling. Some move from job to job; nothing seems to get them down. When the professional survivor has finally come to the end of the road and there are no more places to go, he is calmly prepared for the next step. Don't let this happen to your coaching career.

Referee

The referee is in full charge of the game to ensure the rules and regulations are followed to the letter without fear or favor. The referee is also responsible for controlling starts and stops in the game in collaboration with the official time keeper in the match.
Stoppage time is a common occurrence in American Football. It is occasioned by play of the ball out of designated area, incomplete passes, plus the 3 minute time out allowed for each time in the four quarter sessions in the game.

In addition, there is the official time out when play is halted to set the records straight over dispute ruling. Dispute over distance of ball movement beyond the 10 yard mark is resolved by literal measurement using measuring device to determine the distance. This process gobbles away precious minutes in the game.

The clock has to be resent on completion of this exercise to give the two teams' equal share and opportunity of playtime to commensurate the full duration allocation.
The referee is the main man of the moment during these exercises to make sure the clock is resent and restarted once the ball is in the right place (spotted).

Spectator's Special Day Out

American Football draws crowds to the stadium as circus to attendees. The only difference, circus goers set their own standards and compete with no one on the ground. However, the frequency of activities is just as demanding as in American Football.
Another reason, American football is popular with the masses, spectators have a field day to stand, yell, make waves, sing and dance all in support of the favorite team.

Football match is not a game without spectators from the two competing teams outdoing each other cheering their teams to victory. If spectator's seats are unoccupied, the game is dull. You've never heard original swear words until you sit through the four quarters in football game. Spectators' repertoire of encouraging and sneering words is huge. This is one of the activities that bring football game full circle.

Football stadium is a good place to release steam. However, the spectators are confined within certain perimeters in the stadium. Supporters of one team group together. It is unheard of for a diehard supporter of his/her team to pitch camp in the opponents' team supporters' area. It is difficult but not impossible. Spectators in the game of football change positions from plastic blue, red, green or whatever color of seats in the stadium and standing. What if you can't attend the game live? Does that mean you miss out on the fun? Not if you take into consideration four freaky advantages of watching football live on television.

Four Freaky Advantages of Watching Football on Television

You're not able to attend this season's super bowl, so you settle down to watch the game live on television. You wonder if the thrill of the game will be the same on television as it is in the field with live cheering crowd in the background. What are the advantages of watching football on television?

1. Lines are emphasized on television screen making the line of scrimmage visible. Ball position stand in close up camera shots in the game is enhanced you even see the patches on it and that it sweet.

2. Sound quality is marvelous if you've surround state of the art in sound equipment. If you get close enough you hear the sound of player's foot kicking the ball. That is something you miss on the field. Yes you see them live on the field but from a far and the unmistakable sound of kick on the ball is lost in the ambience of the field.

3. You can hear the referee's voice. What a treat? He is hooked to the sound system which is relayed live to you. Wow! What a feeling. That is something you can only dream about in football field.

4. Instant Replay - Nothing comes close to the excitement of watching every detail of attack, ball fumble and the face of a player who just scored six points on touch with instant replay on television close up shot.

If it's live, it's Sports World!

Wimbledon has lots in common with the Sanchez stadium in Seville or Austria Vienna's luxurious ground in the heart of the prosperously

Austria capital. These stadiums represent milestones in a football journalist career and each holds a wealth of completely separate, fond and funny memories of the game.

Do you ever take notice of commentators perched up in the little boxes on top of the stadium minting words as they watch the game on free of charge ticket courtesy of the newspaper, station? Is that part of job incentives?

If you ever imagined attending the super bowl, here is your free ticket to the game. Become a sports writer.

How times change! In a short time in the field, you can argue acrimoniously with your superiors over the amount to claim for a luxury ride to attend the super bowl game. This is the same thread which tenuously draws many sports writers to this game. Sports writers have such diverse memories and experience of the game compared to spectators and players.

Super Bowl tournament in New York might be as far removed from European football cup finals in Wimbledon as Las Vegas is from Lagos, but the two games generate excitement, elation and chronic disappointment in equal measure no matter where you're and at what level the game is played. That initial magnetic attraction remains undiminished throughout the years of your writing career.

That is not to say there are no moments of discomfort for players, spectators and sports reporters. When you're pinned against the back of the stadium by Seahawks quarter back upset at being described as being flat footed as a penguin," you feel the heat under the collar of your shirt.

Sports Writer

A literary editor always knows when autumn is around the corner. The carpet is strewn thick with humorous statistical offerings from Guinness Book of Records, snippets from past football events, covering them all like a rich top dressing, the annual garnering from the newspaper strips. The public don't expect all these things to come out in the super bowl report, but mention of activities here and there spice the game including the pride of the place – venue of the game.

One of the joys of being involved with football is meeting the game's colorful characters in real life. Men like Ronald Ronny, set being a professional footballer way ahead of his duties as a citizen of United States. On one sorrowful journey back from yet anoth er thrashing for Denver Broncos, the whole ghastly game was redeemed by the man's innate humor. The old coach had lurched round a tight bend to whisper something in Ronny's ear during the dying minutes in the game. In close examination you could tell the coach had issued the unforgettable admonishment to Ronny on the reserve bench.

Then there was Keith Green, long suffering secretary of American football league charged with the onerous task of collecting the players' wages from bank account so terminally overdrawn that the International Monetary Fund would have been frightened by it.

Vivid memories tied to the game of football would make a diehard fan taste the salt of his eyes if he fails to attend the real game live. Inevitably, some of the best memories of sports writers come from days of scratching around in football lower echelons, where the pressures are never quite as intense and the hovering specter of impending doom is no source of comfort to the heart.

You gaze out from the hilltop perched across the plain shimmering in the bright sunlight to get a good panoramic view of this glorious sport.

Different View Points

The fun, aside, the technicalities of the job differ vastly from high school to college and super Bowl football tournaments. In most cases the reporter enjoys the top of the pitch view in the game. Identifying the players is fairly simple job, especially as doubts can be cleared up by turning to a colleague and asking,

"Who is the idiot that kicked that ridiculous back pass?"

On the whole, American football offers such variety you would be mad to miss attending if for nothing else but the luxury to wind up in a sporting event on a free gate   pass. Different Grandstands are separated from the pitch by Olympic size running tracks a nd the broadcasting position can be perched high enough to give you dizziness.

Sorry if the man next to you does not speak English. It is while watching American football at such grounds that you realize a trip to the optician on your return journey home might be a good idea. The pressure of covering Super bowl final can become quite intense. You feel the tension building up with every busload of supporters that arrive in the hosting city, starting from the morning of the match. But the humor is never far and its presence unites the inner knots in an instant. You never forget the contribution to that end from sports writer colleagues.

"The Broncos quarter back would appear to be the first man to come out of the game with aches and pains all over the body," one reporter leans over to whisper in the others ear.

A guy walks past in front of you blocking your vision for a moment. You want to scream because the crowd is up on their feet. You just missed the spectacular touchdown when the guy clad in b lack leather jacket swaggered past and blocked you from the climax of the action in the field.

On the left hand side of the field, St John ambulance men are standing waiting with the studied boredom born of a hundred grazed knees at greyhound tracks, scalds at the speedway, and rope burn wounds to be tended.

Not Many are on Job Assignments

Half a dozen Tom Joneses are up and about to the toilet, to buy drinks and stretch the legs. 22 players are sweating profusely in the field while spectators are rubbing their hands together to keep warm. There is movement all around. Players pick themselves up from being mowed down by opponents as a lady hoist on a six inch stiletto gallivants across the steps of the stadium in a skimpy dress showing a lot of flesh.

You never regret having attended American football match for one moment. Anyone who has had their extremities of frostbite in cold weather will fully appreciate what many only read about and not witness first hand if you're in attendance.

Strangely, footballers don't seem to differ that much whether they are making a fortune from signing up with the major super league or getting equivalent of pocket change the big guys earn in the game earn in high school or college.

Others

Who have we left out? The ball boys and the team doctor will have their space in another publication.

Summary

This chapter credits the success of football game to five other individuals apart from the player. These five individuals include but not exclusive to the coach, referee, sports writer, spectators and mentions ball boys and the team doctors. You don't read about these characters in any football books.

Three chapters 6 on individual player, 8 on five other contributing individuals to the game and chapter nine gives a foretaste of individual successful career in football.

Chapter Nine

THE ULTIMATE SUCCESS IN FOOTBALL GAME

Football team is made up of Individual players. Quarter back, 5 Linesmen, 2 Side Receivers, I Running Back, 1 Full Back and 1 Tight End crew in football team of eleven players squad work play the game in collaboration to advance the ball towards the opponents' end zone.

You can't talk about football match in isolation without giving credit to all those involved in making the game a success. You don't hear much about team doctors and ball boys, yet without them the game would lack in some way.

You see the coach up and about, hear him yell on top of his voice and watch players go after each other and the one with the ball running as if all the demons of hell are after him. Then you've the spectators. Imagine football game without spectators roaring with cheers, making waves, singing along some old tunes during the game to fend off boredom during dry spells when the action is low.

Back to Football Basics

"Back to Basics" sounds, sweet and sensible slogan to rev up support for the super bowl game. You can combine talent and time for the treasure hunt of winning in the game. These three elements form the foundation of winning football game.

• Time Management

Preparation for penalty shootouts nibbles on the game time. There is no time set aside for injury in the game as each case is diffident and unique in nature. The two main clocks keep playtime in check and prevent loss of time and delays during unexpected stoppage time during session of the game.

Time taken by medics to remove injured player from the field could take up to five minutes. In the meantime, play is out.
American football runs on separate stop clocks, play clock to regulate game time, while a second clock is kept to reset and restart in the run up to count down in the match.

Official football game lasts an hour. This period of time is divided up into 4 quarters of 15 minutes each for NFL and 12 minutes duration for high school football. The energy spend by players in the game is greater compared to other physical exercises, jogging, walking, cycling. That explains the short interval duration playtime of quarter hour to take breaks and get re-energized for the next session with vigor and renewed enthusiasm because football players need all the need in the game.

You need the extra energy to subject the body to extreme human combat and brutal attacks as witnessed in American Football.

• Talent

You've the talent. Put it to good use. .

• Treasure

You're in the game to get the job done. That is what every dedicated football player aims. In the real game situation, not all things work out the way you expect. You also don't go sleep as amateur football player and wake the next morning a champion. You diligently train to get in shape and acquire strategy and skills to match required standard of play set by your predecessors in football game. . Here are six simple steps to spur strategy and skills in the game.

Seven Simple Steps to Spur Success Steam

Team work is witnessed in varying degrees in different places. Nature shows the way. Bees, the smallest livestock work as a united team to collect nectar, build hives and protect the queen bee. Dare you invade the territory of these small insects? The army of bees will turn on you with a vengeance stinging one after another.

Coordinating and leading a team to play in harmony and with one accord as the bees call for concerted efforts of players, coach and team officials.

The closest team spirit among human beings is when a country is under siege by the enemy and national security is under threat. The country under attach fight back using all the ammunition at their disposal.

A similar scenario plays in football game. The offense goes all out to harass the defense. The defense feeling threatened hit back with scathing attacks to keep the offense from breaking into their guarded territory. "Over our dead bodies," is the silent mantra the defense provokes in that heat of the moment in the game?

No defense will sit on the fence and let the offense walk all over them to score. The offense must mount a rigorous attack knowing there is equal defense counter attack resistance. Strategies in chapter four come handy to the offense to weaken the defense line up. That said, it is the individual player's contribution that carries the day in the game to win.

"Good timber does not grow with ease, the stronger the wind, the stronger the trees," J. Williard Marrot said. These words reflect the meaning of life from both nature and logic. From a logical stand point, the harder the work, the better and bigger is the outcome.

What do you do as an individual player to make the game a success? Here are five things that make individual contribution in the game yield tangible expected results.

1. **Set Yourself Free**.

If you allow negative thoughts from previous game run and rule your life, you might as well not play at all. You cannot let negative thoughts take over and steer the decision making mechanism – the brain during the game. That would narrow your horizon in the match and confine you to a life of defeat. Breathe new life in to the game with positive mental attitude by setting the records straight in the mind.

Set yourself free from negative mental attitude. Stimulate the process of winning the game by focusing on the outcome and stand firm.

2. **Stand Firm**

You've equal 24 hours to the day, seven days a week. Stakeholders, coach and officials of the game are prepared to walk you through school, college, super bowl tournament competition. Enormous resources have been used to purchase the gear to protect you from injury. You get that covered in chapter three. Your part is to commit time, talent to lift the treasured trophy of the game in an hour.

The passion to succeed in life is inherent in every one, you included. Resolve to stand firm against stiff competition posed by the opponents in the game and your effort will pay off. Recall past successful encounters to memory to inspire you.

3. **Summon Past Successful Experience.**

Think of an incident in the past game that made a difference in your team. Hold on to that thought resolutely as you battle it out with opponents in the field. You did then. You can do it again now without carving under pressure. Stay focused on the ultimate price to lift the trophy.

4. **Visualize Victory in Advance**

No matter the difficulties challenges, a barrage of attack by opponents, resolve never to retreat or surrender. Soldier on to take control of the ball and position in the field and the victory comes into sharp focus of your vision

You're unhappy with your dismal performance in the first quarter of the game. Tap into the reservoir of past successful experiences and get into flow of the game with assistance of team mates. Learn the benefits of this move towards the end of this section.

5. Success Satisfaction

"Success is simple. First, you decide what you want specifically, second you decide you are willing to pay the price to make it happen, and then pay the price," Bunker Hunt, the Texas billionaire said. Sample the following four stimuli steps to improve quality performance in playing football.

Four Stimulus Steps to Improve Quality Performance

If you bumped on Ronny on the streets of Las Vegas, you would confuse him for club or traditional casino bouncer. Ronny stands at 6' 7." He has broad shoulders, deep blue eyes, trim waistline, wears white head band on black thick hair during football game. What difference would Ronny's late entrance during the dying minutes of the game make?

The most striking feature in his body is his biceps. You think they are swollen by the look on them. Ronny also prefers to wear short sleeve shirts and T-shirts which enhance the size of his arms. Why do most big boned bouncers wear short sleeve shirts? You get the message from physique. "Don't mess with Ronny."

You've got to get close to know Ronny is humane and humble outside of the football pitch. Ronny didn't need to work hard pumping away and lifting weights at the gym to get his athletic body in shape and size. His lanky size is part of inheritance from his father's genes. He looked 10 years older than the rest of his peers in high school. That is also the reason football coaches sought and recruited him in this game. Ronny doesn't disappoint. He makes good use of his body size and shape to mow down opponents on the field.

In addition to the football gear you're minced meat taking Ronny head on in this game.

Ronald Ronny started practicing to perfect football play at age 7. He won many coaches admiration in high school. This gave him a wide range of choice of scholarships into the best colleges supportive of Football in the United States of America. Ronny is one of many successful stories. What makes one player stand out in the team? How does diversity of individual participants in the game forge unity in the team?

Self Imposed Hindrance to Fruitful Football Career

The single biggest hindrance to success in any field is in the mind. Everyone could do with an overhaul of the human brain, not literally as in car engine parts pulled apart. Making headway in life requires you change the way you think from negative to positive. It is as simple as that, yet so hard it eludes many well meaning people to excel in preferred field of preference.

Napoleon Hill uses the following quote to illustrate the place and power of the mind in the life and history of human beings.

"Our greatest precious natural resource is not our mineral deposits or beautiful forests. It's the mental attitude and the imagination of people of every generation… Our real wealth is the intangible power of thought."

You're now good and ready to take on opponents in the game of foot ball driven by a desire to win and assisted by team mates, and coach. Spice these four stimulus steps and you're home and dry at the end of the super bowl game with a resounding win over opponents. Nothing works in favor of success as self determination to attain the ultimate prize. This section draws your attention to four stimulus steps to improve quality performance.

1. Develop Sense of Direction.

"A journey of a thousand miles begins with the first step," A Chinese proverb says. The two competing football teams in super bowl visualize victory in advance. That is what keeps the team spirit high and alive when the tough gets going. Having a positive mental attitude creates vivid mental picture of the actions individual t eam members need engage the opponents in running battles for the battle.

If the team set out to win, pulling off the super bowl game is within reach. If the team is wavers and doubt wrecks havoc in their hearts, it is a done deal defeat from the word go. This is the Unique Selling Point of this book. This crucial proposition is given emphasis in chapter six. Small wonder, world class super bowl teams engage the services of qualified motivational speakers to improve players self confidence and performance.

The actual physical game in the field is the outward demonstration of the inward desire of each member of the team to win. Most NFL games play out in the minds of individuals players long be fore the players set foot on the field.

2. Draw from the Well that never runs Dry – Brain

You can feel, touch and taste the sweetness of success all around the field. You've got what it takes to collaborate with other team members to show the opponents your team is the champion of the match this season.

3. Disengage the Mind from Past Poor Performances.

The way to get around separating good from bad data in the brain is to reprogram it. That is the secret of success in the brain battle. Negative thoughts of losing will invade your brain and position themselves to takeover. You can choose to quarantine harmful thoughts and gain mastery of the mind by disengaging the mind from past poor performances. Make your thoughts become the driving force in the game.

4. Driven by Success

Your body and brain will repel each other and go on slow motion, if you don't harmonize the head and the heart in dealing with negative metal attitude - emotions and feeling.

You've a wonderful body system and superb brain. It's time you rethink about playing football in the context of the big picture. Big picture thinking changes present result oriented to future purpose driven performance. This is the running theme through out this book.

Purpose driven quality performance does not only come from super bowl game "Think Tanks." Individual players' performances in the game hold the key that unlocks doors of opportunity to win with a huge margin. Purpose driven performance is the declaration of the end from the beginning. What are the benefits of emphasis on individual player's performance?

Six Benefits associated with Individual Participation in the Game.

1. Lifts the team from the pits.

The team could be reeling under pressure of time and trailing 10-21 in the game. The best hope to gain extra point in a touchdown to make the score 16-21depends on attitude and performance.
You can change the matrix in the game with 2 point conversion to lift them out of the pits of despair and eventual defeat. Although the score is not evened out with this single move, 3 point deficit could be achieved by one field goal kick. The downside in this case is failure to secure the deficit. That is why it is important that the team visualizes victory outcome throughout the game. Six point score to put the team in the lead does not come from negative but positive mental attitude.

2. Touch Down is a Milestone Score.

1984 Orange Super Bowl failed attempt to secure the two points conversion cost Nebraska a dear loss. In 2007, overtime play yielded a win from a 2 point conversion for the first time. Here is how it works.

3. Defense gains control of the ball and advances into the opponents end zone by blocking, intercepting or receiving the ball from a fumble, the result earn the team 2 points on secure touchdown.

4. In the event the opponent scores a safety, the team is awarded 2 points, although this is rare in the game.
5. Game Clock Advancement

Delays occasioned by different activities in the game are compensated for by advancing the game clock but maintaining the play time in the game. The two exceptions to this rule are: -

- A team scores on touchdown during sudden death overtime bringing the game to a satisfying close.
- Any of the two teams in possession of the ball could score on touch to take the lead in which case its game short. – Bull's Eye. The team that gets possession of the ball benefits when official signals for a free kick award on punt, place, drop kick at 20 yard line from the opponents end zone.

Summary

You get snippets of individual involvement in the game of football throughout this book. Chapter six offers exclusive information on individual football player. In this chapter the emphasis on individual participation comes full circle. It is back to basics with time management, talent search, and treasure hunt in this lucrative sports event career. How do you go about all these?

Take seven simple steps to spur football steam, spice them with four stimulus steps to improve quality performance and the ultimate price you get is six benefits associated with individual participation in football game.

Good Luck!

The next chapter ten gives you a summary of twenty one commonly used terms in football a simple explanation. If in the process of reading through the book you did not get a grasp one term and need to refresh your memory with the term this chapter is for you.
If you need to quickly go over the terms in readiness of the game but don't have time to read the whole book, chapter ten will get you up and running in the game in no time. The terms are in alphabetical order to making your search easy and fast.

Chapter Ten

TERMS COMMONLY USED IN FOOTBALL GAME

1. Coin Flip

Coin flip determines kick off at the start of the game. Each session in the game starts with the winning team taking the kick off. In addition to the 3 minute break in case of tie at the end of normal playtime. There are two minute interval breaks for each team to score in the absence of touchdown in the extra time in the game.

2. Dead Ball

When is the ball considered dead? Ten reasons that cause deal ball situation.

- The player having the ball is put down to the ground.
- Incomplete pass – The ball falls to the ground before the next player gets a hold of it.
- Player or ball comes in contact with side line, considered off the mark on the pitch – "Out of Bounds."
- Ball hits goal posts except during field scoring attempt.
- Team scores on touchdown kick off.
- Fair catch – signified by waving hands above the head by player. This signal denotes he has been manhandled contrary to set rules and regulations of the game.
- Downing
- Kicked ball rests during ball play before reaching the end zone or "spotted."
- In the case of touch back.
- Ball in play recovered by a different player.

- The ball is touched by player before the 10 yard space areas of coverage during kick off.

In any of these cases, the game official nearest the place of action blows the whistle to alert players, the ball is dead.

3. Defense

In soccer, volleyball and basketball matches, coaches call time to change pattern of play, regroup the teams. During this period the coach gives instruction on the next course of action, defense need to keep opponents at bay. This is also an opportunity to for players to grab and gulp down a bottle of water, breathe before assuming another session of grueling task to find the back of opponents net with the ball.

4. Downed Play

You hear and read about workers strikes and the phrase commonly used is that the workers "downed their tools." You can draw a number of parallel inferences from this phrase in connection to NFL. "Downed," implies as the name suggests take down. You don't need proof or further explanation of this word in American Football. Watch the game and see the word demonstrated in action.

5. Fair Catch – NFL Only 3 Points Score

Fair catch is the only free kick that earns 3 points in NFL. The procedure is similar in nature to other kicks offs where the ball is held firmly to the ground in preparation to for the kick off exercise by a member of the team. It could also be drop, tee. The desired sure score destination is that the ball is kicked to pass through the two goal posts. This is the only time a free kick score 3 points and the kick passes between the two goal posts under the steel bar.

6. Scrimmage Downs

Activities in the game revolve around plays, down, beginning at the line of scrimmage in the field. Ball play starts by official in the game placing the ball on a designated spot on the ground of marked football field.

7. Sudden Death

Sudden death rule is observed in a tie situation during the 15 minutes extra time awarded for play on top of the normal official game duration of one hour. If none of the two teams score the game ends in a draw.

In 2010 NFL revised and modified sudden death rule in American Football. In the new system, two teams get equal ball possession opportunity excerpt in the case one team scores a touchdown in the period to win the game outright. In the new sudden death system the two teams have a go at ball possession by punt, kick off or touchdown to gain win advantage. If both use up respite time without score the game ends in a tie.

The sudden death rule is not always cut and dry. A number of activities could foul up the process and change the normal course of direction in the game. For example, in post season multiple renewable 15 minutes overtime interval periods were played in the period 2011-2012 NFL between Denver Broncos and Pittsburg Steelers in Denver Colorado state.

Denver Broncos won with an 80 yard touchdown in the first overtime play from Tim to Thomas

8. Neutral Zone

Neutral Zone is the narrow strip width around football pitch earmarked only for snapper. Players are considered out of bound in this stretch. Think of neutral zone in terms of No Man's Land between country boundaries. None of the two adjacent countries own that piece of land yet they share it a common ground for contact.

9. Pattern of Play

Players in all competitive games practice the pattern to be followed in the actual game to gain control of the game and outdo opponents.

In maintaining balance and enhancing competitive advantage, teams conform to strict rules which define and identify their unique pattern of play to move the ball forwards or backwards. The pattern consists of seven players lining up on the line and for directly behind the line of scrimmage. This formation allows room for six receivers of the forward ball pass. Receivers comprise running back full back and tight end.

In college football, ineligible receivers are identified by Jersey numbers 50-79 while receivers wear 48 or 80-99 Jersey numbers.

10. Starting Downs

American Football movement in the game starts when the ball is thrown by a snapper who could also hand it to one of the backs in his team preferably quarterback. Quarter back in turn can handle, throw or run with the ball towards the end zone for touchdown. If the ball is dead, that calls for it to be spotted to engineer new play session. In the event the referee calls out for incomplete pass, the ball is taken back to where play previously went out of hand.

11. Free Kick Offs

The kicking team is expected to stand behind the ball whereas the receiving team should be 10 yards down the file when the free kick off is taken. One, free kick is taken with the ball on tee (held and the kicking team lined up 35 yards line. This distance safeguards collision of players in the scramble for the ball. The space created allows for room to engage one another at safe distance with reduced force in running and covering that distance.

12. Other Kicks

Free kicks are awarded in the game when the ball is dead for whatever reasons other than the ones mentioned in the previous paragraph. The team under pressure held hostage in their end zone gets the opportunity to kick the ball from 20 yards line. This is called a place kick, drop, or punt.

13. Scoring

Score in football is awarded points ranging from 1-6 depending on the type of score and the position of the ball is kicked from or handled. Touchdown attracts the highest score on the scale earning the team a whooping six points at ago.

Three points is awarded the team for scoring a field goal with place, drop or free kick from a fair catch. Most of the time, the place kick is commonly used to earn the 3 points score. In each of these kicks, the ball must cross the goal line above the two steel goal posts. If the kick misses the mark, the ball is returned to the original place where the kick was taken to resume play referred to as the scrimmage line. The official standing under the goal posts signals by extending both hands in outward vertical position above his head when a score is made. The scoring team also kicks off the ball on the next playtime phase.

14. Touch Downs

Touchdowns earn teams the maximum 6 points on the score card in the game. Touchdown is the every football player's ultimate aim. When you maneuver, outrun and cross the imaginary line on the opponents' side with the ball in hand to place the ball down on the end zone, beyond the goal line, you achieve a feat many only dream about in American Football. How does a player manage to outrun opponents?

A player could outrun opponents' from any point in the field, cease the opportunity to close the short distance to the end zone from a pass to place a touchdown and bag in six points straight up in the game. These three ways warrant a perfect score of six to show for the efforts in the game.

15, Touchdown

Touchdown is worth six points, scored when a player receives the ball from a teammate while he is in the end zone, or carries the ball to the end zone. When a player scores a touchdown, his attacking team has the chance to kick the football for a bonus point. For a successful kick, the ball has to pass between the two upright posts.

16. Winning

The winner of the game is the team with the highest points after the final whistle. In case of a tie, over time is included where the opposing teams play for an extra quarter until there is a winner. Whether you're a spectator, sports writer, coach, ball boy team doctor, whatever your contribution to the game big or small, the team's win is your win too. So the ultimate win belongs to the individual.

17. Controller

You need good field position and ball control in the game of football to advance play.
All the efforts and attempts to block the offense or penetrate the human defense wall would amount to nothing without good position and ball handling.

Whether this position of management is at higher level in government institution or business, expected outcome is the same.

18. Fouls and Penalties

American football game is action packed with lots of body contact. Tempers flare, brutal tackles, calculated moves call for regulation to maintain delicate balance between the two opposing teams. It is inevitable that penalties are put in place and fair punishment muted to sustain the rhythm of the event. The offenders are punished for violating set rules and deliberate acts that cause bodily harm to opponents in the game.

Football would be a massacre not a match if the balance and flow is not checked from time to time. Penalties keep the players in check and make huge differences in the outcome of the game. A foul could mean loss of the game if the other team members use the opportunity to score from kick off awarded for penalty. This is the reason for kick off at 5, 10, 15, 25 yard ranges awarded to aggrieved teams.

Serious cases of fouls can result in a player disqualified to participate in the game and there would no replacement. This is more devastating for the team would play with fewer men making it more difficult to contain the opponents' full squad of 11. There is bound to be cracks in the lineup of the team severely penalized for fouls in this way. Playing the game one match down adds more pressure on top of contending with the competition at an equal playing field.

Morale is likely to wane and the high spirit steam the team started on could be compromise giving way to poor performance hence eventual los of the game in a humiliating defeat.

Reason to take advantage of the deficit in the opponents' side would prevail among the favorite team to mount rigorous attacks and hit the opponents at their weakest point of the missing team member in the game. Another disadvantage to the punished team would be the penalty shootout awarded in lieu of the offense. Not many teams would think twice to decline such offers to widen the lead.

19. Personal Fouls

Personal fouls which pose danger to other players are punished in equal measure in line with the gravity of the foul. The team offended team is awarded 15 yard line penalty kick for personal fouls. Rarely do personal fouls result in ejecting a player from the game, but that does not rule out the possibility.

The most common fouls are holding illegal blocking or personal is awarded with safety

20. Time Out

Football teams benefit from 3 timeouts in the one long game with additional time out periods should the game extend to overtime on tie score.

In soccer, volleyball, basketball matches, coaches call 'Time Out,' for various reasons. If the team is trailing in scores to opponents, a new line of offense needs to be put in place to find the back of the opponents net.

In some cases, time out means change of tactics or pattern of play. Time out in football share similar reasons with variations here and there to suit the game. No team goes into playtime without one goal to win. If the time spent is not bearing fruit, the coach will resort time out in the game. In this short period coach instructs team members on the next course of action in the game.

21. Instant Replay

A mistake is a mistake, whether it is intended or not. The element of human error in making decision during the game necessitates instant replay. Team coaches are allowed to petition up to two decisions in a given game. During which time, the instant replay is watched by officials of the game to ascertain if indeed mistake was made in allowing or not allowing penalty for the action in the game.

The coat signals for instant replay with a red flag, thrown to indicate this process. If the team loses in the petition, they also loose time out in the game. Secure score with two makes the team eligible for third instant replay whose result the referee announces over the wireless microphone.

College football is down to one instant replay challenge in each game. The officer in the box monitors the replay, takes note of errors and alerts the other officials the field for the need of instant replay. The official in the box is responsible for performing instant replay, reviews process and makes final announcement of the outcome.

High school football does not have video clip facility for instant replay and review. Time out is used instead in which the coach and referee discuss and consult widely over the ruling. What is the difference between NFL and college football? How do the differences pale in comparison to the similarities most of which reflect NFL standards?

Let the match begin!

.

CONCLUSION

Thank you again for downloading this book!

I hope this book was able to help you understand football so you're not clueless of what is happening during the game. The next step is to implement what you have learnt when watching the next NFL match.

Finally, if you enjoyed this book, kindly leave a review for this book on Amazon?

Click here to leave a review for this book on Amazon!

Thank you and good luck!

RESOURCES:

1. https://en.wikipedia.org/wiki/American_football_rules

2. https://en.wikipedia.org/wiki/Protective_equipment_in_gridiron_football

3. http://www.forbes.com/sites/shephyken/2016/02/06/five-super-bowl-strategies-to-win-over-yyour-customers/#8a774f25c7a5

4. http://www.dummies.com/how-to/content/how-offense-gains-better-field-position-in-footbal.html

5. http://www.dummies.com/how-to/content/how-an-offense-can-beat-a-defense-in-american-foot.html

6. http://footballsquares.blogspot.co.ke/

7. http://www.sbnation.com/nfl/2015/2/1/7960971/seahawks-patriots-2015-super-bowl-xlix-results-final-score

8. http://espn.go.com/nfl/recap?gameId=340202007   –   Super Bowl 2014

9. Sommer, Bobbe, Psycho-Cybernetics: A Complete Update of Maxwell M   Maltz Classic. New York: Apprentice Hall.

10. Hill, Napoleon, Principles of Success:

11. Waitley, Dennis, The Dynamics of Winning.

Made in the USA
San Bernardino, CA
18 September 2017